The New Eden

The New Eden:

Paradise Retold

By Katherine Hall Newburgh, Ph. D

Copyright © 2022. Katherine Hall Newburgh, Ph. D, and Books of Eden Publishing, LLC.
All Rights Reserved.

ISBN: 979-8-9860446-0-6

Cover Art and Design: Copyright © 2022 by Katherine Hall Newburgh, Ph. D

For Paul.

My greatest hope is that, as you read, you will see the places you would have stepped.

Table of Contents

ACKNOWLEDGEMENTS I
FOREWORD IV
PREFACE VIII
INTRODUCTION 1
   THE GREAT CHANGE 1
   OUR APOTHEOSIS 3
   LEADERSHIP IN THE NEW EDEN 4
   AWAKENING FROM PRISON 7
   THE ROLE OF THE HEART 9
   INTENTIONS AND ROADMAP FOR THIS BOOK 11
      Summary of Part I: Teachings of the New Eden 12
      Summary of Part II: Visualizations for Embodying the New Eden 14
   HOW TO READ THIS BOOK 16
      The Visualizations 16
      Preparing for Change 17
      A Note on Terminology 18

PART I: TEACHINGS OF THE NEW EDEN 20
   CHAPTER 1: EDEN 21
      The Living Memory of Eden 22
      The Personal and the Collective Eden 25
      Awakening to Power 25
      "And the Fruit" 30
      Inner Eden: The Manifest Light of the Soul 49
   CHAPTER 2: AWAKENING 53
      Self and World 55
      Money 62
      Embodiment 64
      Original Sin, Debt, and Redemption 88
      Atonement 98
      Unconditional Love 105
      The Power of the Heart 112

PART II: VISUALIZATIONS FOR EMBODYING THE NEW EDEN 121

INITIATING CONSCIOUS RE-BIRTH 122
An Invitation to Enter 122
Visualization for Sacred Protection 123

CHAPTER 3: PURPOSE 128
Teachings of Purpose 128
Visualization for Embodying Purpose 131

CHAPTER 4: INTEGRITY 138
Teachings of Integrity 138
Visualization for Embodying Integrity 142

CHAPTER 5: EMPTINESS 148
Teachings of Emptiness 148
Visualization for Embodying Emptiness 150

CHAPTER 6: PRESENCE 156
Teachings of Presence 156
Visualization for Embodying Presence 158

CHAPTER 7: TRUST 166
Teachings of Trust 166
Visualization for Embodying Trust 168

CHAPTER 6: SOVEREIGNTY 177
Teachings of Sovereignty 177
Visualization for Embodying Sovereignty 180

CHAPTER 9: DEVOTION 189
Teachings of Devotion 189
Visualization for Embodying Devotion 191

CONCLUSION 200
REFERENCES 202
ABOUT THE AUTHOR 203

Acknowledgements

No book is ever written alone. I gratefully acknowledge these loving human beings who, despite my best efforts, never allowed me to be totally an island. These people supported me unconditionally on my journey, and my words are inadequate to share the depth of my gratitude.

Thank you, Mom and Dad, for loving me and supporting me even when it was hard to understand.

Thank you, Maggie and Ann, for reminding me of what home feels like when I couldn't remember on my own. Thank you also for the space suit, the leather strap with my writing on it, and your gift of the only other book published in Worcester, VT: *The Cow that Tried to Swallow a Potato*.

Thank you, Laura, Eduardo, Bea, and Brinkley for the videos that kept me laughing and kept me going.

Thank you, Murphy, my Buddha Cat, for loving me enough to set me free (or, more accurately, for finally getting fed up enough with my peripatetic lifestyle to leave). I hope you are lounging at this moment surrounded by a very stationary family that feeds you chicken and is as obsessed with you as I was (am).

Thank you, Sam and Yelena, for showing me how to stand in my power. The real medicine was, always and ever, the way that you loved me.

Thank you, Boyd, for guiding me all the way to Inner Earth.

Thank you, Willow, for seeing me as a mountain.

Thank you, Mike Q, for the prayers. I think they are working!

Thank you, Lindsay, Lara, Clara, Marjorie, Julie, Sarah, Bronwyn, and Nina: Goddesses. Beloveds. Friends. Thank you for letting me come and go and for loving me no matter what.

Thank you, Jenn, Robin, and Will for believing in me.

Thank you, Karen, for the tinctures and the snowy winter walks.

Thank you, Kelly, for helping me let go at the crucial moment.

Thank you, Morgan, for holding the magic when I was tempted to doubt.

Thank you, Kira, for unlocking me. Thank you for your unconditional support, and thank you for showing me that the darkness is a nice place to be.

Thank you, Noreen, for never forgetting to check up on me, even (especially) when I was in the womb of creation! Thank you as well for generously proofreading the final version.

Thank you, Mike D., for reminding me of my worth whenever I forgot.

Thank you, Judith, for reminding me again and again of my origin- the mysticism that feels so much like home.

Thank you, Hannah and Tucker, for the walk. I needed your aura of quiet contentment more than you can know.

Thank you, Dr. Mintz for introducing me to Eve all those years ago. She has been with me ever since.

Thank you, Chris and Pat, for providing a beautiful, quiet home for me to create in.

Thank you, Sam and Gus, for being good neighbors and for checking in on me when my car didn't move for days. And, of course, thank you for the chaga! It taught me the ancient secret of patience.

Thank you, Paul, for the long conversations. I've never known anyone who could amplify wisdom like you. We've covered so much terrain, you and I! You believed in me from the start, and just look what we've done!

Finally, thank you to my anonymous benefactor whose generosity allowed me to live and create this legacy. I pray that it brings peace and love, healing, and joy to all.

Foreword
By Kira Krier

I walked into the yoga studio to teach my last noontime Bikram yoga class, as weeks of no one turning up had finally brought the class to a close. I had prepared myself for the empty studio, and to my surprise Kate Newburgh was sitting there, on her mat, waiting for me. It was an instant connection of our souls. We began to talk; there was no "feeling each other out." From the moment we met we both knew our souls had arrived together again after centuries apart. There was never "light conversation;" we moved quickly into talking of healing. I spoke excitedly about the powerful magic of quantum hypnosis healing, and she shared with me her journey with her Heart Imagery work. Our connection was felt deep within our souls. It was a sense of knowing that oftentimes cannot be explained–yet if you have felt it, you know what I am speaking of.

Kate is a brilliant, intuitive, inspirational soul, and this book will take you on the transformative journey that your inner self has been waiting for. You will feel the shift as the wisdom and the truth of Eden is unfolded. *The New Eden* brings the promise to the arrival of peace, harmony, love, and transparency in this lifetime. The chapters take you on a wild ride, exploring the depths of yourself and the meaning of things you have spent decades trying to dismantle. With every turn of a page, you find yourself closer to understanding. Kate draws you into the divine, reminding you throughout the entire book that we are "perfect fractals of the Earth." Reading this will bring a euphoric sense, each word emphasizing that we as humans on this plane are made of divine love.

The New Eden: Paradise Retold is spellbinding and will keep you awake, riveted by every word of knowledge that you have known over many lifetimes. If you are open to receiving the knowledge, your entire body will respond–your inner vibration radiates louder and louder as the truth settles into your bones. The information Kate shares with us in the beginning chapters prepares you for the guided visualizations. The deep dive into healing and understanding our roots is easily accessible through her words. If your conscious mind doesn't remember, the tools Kate has provided will gently lead you to a place of understanding.

When you put the book down for rest you will be filled with joy and understanding. By the last page you will see yourself as the divine being you were always meant to be.

This book evokes the powerful messages of the likes of Kahlil Gibran and Pema Chödrön. Kate leans into her own higher consciousness and directly connects to Source/God/Divine to deliver these powerful messages to us. Kate gives us this offering with a profound confidence and assurance that will embrace you in its light. *The New Eden* gives you knowledge and tools so you too can access this place of Eden, this Paradise. Deep within the cells of your body you will experience the cleansing and opening it needs. You will know it, you will feel it, in every word, as it speaks to your higher consciousness and awakens the pieces that were once sleeping.

Oftentimes I have heard you speak of one who commits a wrong as though he were not one of you, but a stranger unto you and an intruder upon your world.
But I say that even as the holy and the righteous cannot rise beyond the highest which is in each one of you,
So the wicked and the weak cannot fall lower than the lowest which is in you also.
And as a single leaf turns not yellow but with the silent knowledge of the whole tree,
So the wrong-doer cannot do wrong without the hidden will of you all...

And if any of you would punish in the name of the righteousness and lay the axe unto the evil tree, let him see to its roots;
And verily he will find the roots of the good and the bad, the fruitful and the fruitless, all entwined together in the silent heart of the Earth.

-Kahlil Gibran, *The Prophet*

Eden is upon us! Our apotheosis is in our very next breath. Let us celebrate! Let us

> *…pluck til time and times are done*
> *The silver apples of the moon*
> *The golden apples of the sun.*

-Yeats (with help from me)

Preface

Three years ago, in December 2018, I died. It was a terrifying thing, death. The last thing I remember is my head hitting the floor of an empty, cavernous meeting hall in Salt Lake City. It was the middle of the night, and I was alone.

I have heard of walk-ins, of souls switching places in a living body. It is possible this is what happened to me, though I cannot be certain. All I know is that after that night, everything changed. Within weeks I had quit my job. I stopped seeing friends and loved ones. The world had become a bewildering place, and those I loved seemed like strangers to me. I couldn't relate to the person I had been, the life I had lived, the world I had moved in, or the ambitions I had harbored. The life I'd come from seemed small and far away, as though it belonged to someone else, someone unrecognizable to me.

I spent the following three years learning how to come back to life. I finally accepted that I lived in a new world, one that not many could see. I wrote this book because I didn't know how to explain it to anyone- this new world I was living in.

I spent the final year before the publication of this book living in almost unbroken solitude. In that year I traveled from place to place, country to country. I fasted from the reality that others seemed to live in. This was not a gesture of asceticism or renunciation- it was move of protection. My whole being felt like the skin underneath a broken fingernail- so tender that the slightest touch was exceedingly painful. In many ways, I was free for the first time in my life, and I was also more lost than I had ever been. I became extremely quiet. There was nowhere to turn but inwards, no one to lean on but the forces I couldn't see. I couldn't see them, couldn't prove their existence, but I could feel them. I could hear them.

Sometimes I awoke to the sound of bells, ringing as clearly as though they were in the same room. These bells- they were the celestial spheres, the chimes of Sophia. They pealed like silver, like bright laughter in that liminal space between waking and dreaming.

I was born in the Midwest where farmers would often string a rope between house and barn so that they would be able to find their way in a blizzard. In the three years after my awakening, this book became my rope, my thread, my lifeline, the one solid thing that could guide me. No matter where I was, as long as I was writing, I was home.

The first draft of this book, completed two years ago in the mountains of Colorado during deep winter, would be unrecognizable to you, just as I would have been unrecognizable to you if you were to meet me then. The book always knew what it wanted to be, and it had the patience to wait for me to evolve into the person who could write it. I had to grow into my convictions, learn the power of my beliefs. I had to practice these beliefs so that they became natural, stronger than the clamoring world- so brash and unrepentant in its relentless declaration of reality.

I learned to believe in the strange synchronicities, the miraculous interventions, the uncanny coincidences that kept occurring in my life. The more I leaned on my faith, the more it supported me. It could not be explained, only lived. Only witnessed. Only received. I documented some of these miracles in a memoir, but there are far, far more of them than I could possibly record. I believed in the bells, you see. I believed they were real, though no one else could hear them. How to explain this, without sounding mad?

I saw how miracles manifested, sometimes through the most unexpected means, sometimes through mundane occurrences, no less breathtaking for being simple. And this, I saw, was the other side to miracles. How to explain to someone a miracle had occurred when it could easily be brushed away? I tell you, just because something can be explained doesn't mean it's not magic.

I have awakened, and I speak to you from the space of becoming- this liminal place between awakening and completion. I do not profess to know all. I offer here only that which I have touched on, experienced, felt, but have not yet fully become. I know that we live in a world of magic so far beyond what we can imagine. I know that we are capable of so much more than we can possibly comprehend. Magic is real, and it is among us. It is within us. The power of our collective belief has given rise to a world riven with fear, but this isn't where it ends. Somewhere within us, we understand that there is a transcendent sphere, a place we can access that brings all into harmony. We know that this story, *our story,* will not end in heartbreak.

As divine beings, we are capable of creating any reality we want. As a divine collective, we are capable of creating a world founded on generosity, love, abundance, joy. This is possible and much, much simpler than any of us could possibly imagine.

No reference to the phenomenal world, which is ephemeral and fleeting, can offer a foundation for the future we are stepping into. Our state of consciousness is evolving beyond what we have ever known. Therefore, that which I draw from to write this book leaves behind established "data" that can be measured and conceived of by the rational mind. As it is this very mind we are transcending, we cannot use it to comprehend how to live, act, and be in the world that is upon us. For that feat, we require a much more powerful instrument.

I refer, of course, to the heart.

The heart is our redemption and our grace. It is the part of us that never forgets its divine origin, and it is our unfailing guide to the New Eden that is upon us. In many ways, this book offers a pathway to realizing your divinity. It is a shout from the labyrinth, an epistle from someone who is - maybe just ahead, maybe just behind- walking with you the mazy passageways of shadow and light to arrive, finally, in the sanctuary of our collective heart.

There are many of us who walk between worlds. I am one of these people and yet I hold no world above the other. It is true that I tried to escape this world, the one of bewildering cruelty, of suffering and pain. I moved from place to place, person to person, house to house, community to community, trying to find somewhere, anywhere on Earth that was free of pain and weakness and cruelty. At times, I wanted very much to leave altogether. In my travels, I accepted, finally, there is nowhere on Earth untouched by suffering. In that moment of revelation, I discovered something else. I learned I hadn't come here to escape. I came here to witness the world, engage with it, love it, and move among it as a beacon, a living sun on Earth, as someone emanating an undeniably human gift. And so, too, have you.

Since the beginning, this book has lived within me as an unnameable question. I have journeyed along the thread of this question for so very long, arriving here, once again, at the shores of rebirth. This book is alchemical in nature. It was drawn into being from unseen places. It offers the subtle and simple transmission of those places. This book is serious and loving and holds the aching poignancy of being human. And yet, with all of its earnestness and passion, with all of its innocent declarations, it defies cynicism. I cannot hold this book in anything but reverence: the simple offering of someone split apart by love.

The answer, after all, is simple. We could jump right to it. But what would be the fun in that? We came here to live our own story. This, Reader, is mine.

Introduction

The Great Change

You will have noticed, perhaps, that things are changing?

Some speak of a time when we will go back to "the way things were," but such is not the path of evolution. In our lives, and as a collective, we must accept that there is no going back. The universe is not interested in repeating what has been. And neither, if we are to be truly honest with ourselves, are we.

A new era is upon us- one where our old assumptions and ways of operating will no longer function. Those who look to the past as their guide will become lost, bewildered, and increasingly fearful as all they've ever known, everything that has ever "worked" ceases to yield what it once did. Humanity is in the midst of a great leap and all of the Earth along with it.

The shift upon us is no less than an upheaval of the foundational assumption of evolution. Up until now, as a species we have been focused on adapting for survival. The time we are in however- the time of the Great Change- heralds a shift from evolving to *survive* to evolving to *thrive*.

True thriving, as we will see, is beyond the scope of our rational mind to understand. It is not a thoughtform that that can be rationalized. Instead, thriving is a state of being that must be felt within the body itself. Thriving is a state beyond fear, beyond limitation, and beyond *reason* that demands an entirely different way of knowing the world- one where the mind has relaxed fully in service to the heart.

As of now, very few human beings have achieved this state of thriving. It is, however, ready to come upon our species like a wave for those who are open and ready to receive it. In this new era of consciousness, body, mind, and spirit will unite in a state of perfect harmony wherein nothing is denied, nothing is rejected, and nothing within us is at war. Such is the state of the New Earth. Such is thriving. Such is the gift of the New Eden.

The leap of consciousness offered in this time is not dependent upon anything but an open mind and willing heart. Any human anywhere can receive this gift. It requires only that you ask for it, humbly and in earnest. When you ask, you will receive it in exactly the way that is right for you.

Movement into this new realm of consciousness is initiated when we finally confront our fear of death. This confrontation moves our awareness from the attempt to elude death (i.e., a focus on survival) to living the gift of our lives to the utmost. Lifting ourselves up and out of our fear of death means tapping into the plane that exists beyond death. We must move our consciousness into the part of our being that is not dependent on the perpetually unstable world of form. This place/sphere/realm/ aspect of being is what I refer to as "the divine," and it exists already within each of us.

In this coming era, we will co-create with our eternal divine nature to ensure that our beautiful human body - this exquisite and fleeting expression of the soul- and the rich tapestry of our life, reach the height of their most fulfilling, most joyful expression. We will learn that this is absolutely possible despite all of the harsh and blunt factors on the planet that tell us otherwise. We learn, in fact, that anything and everything is possible. We will learn that our ultimate flourishing is not a matter of effort, will, or discipline, but of surrender, trust, and acceptance.

By standing on that higher rung- the realm of being that is not dependent on form- we will finally stop making death into a problem so we can get on with the business of living. As we accept the ephemeral nature of form, our fears, our constrictions, our caution, and our self-deception wither away in the face of our exuberant desire to accept this life in all of its richness and depth.

The New Eden is a state of thriving. It blooms and flourishes now. It invites us to trust in this life and its capriciousness. It offers the joy that moves us through darkness into the birthright of our highest fulfillment.

Our Apotheosis

Up until now, the word "human" has been synonymous with limitation, with conflict, with suffering and pain. When we refer to the "human" aspect of ourselves, we invariably mean that which we believe to be flawed. We refer to that which sabotages our happiness and success. We say, "that's just the human in me." We shrug sheepishly and excuse our weakness, our doubt, our inner turmoil as "human."

We sell ourselves short. Conflict and fear, doubt, regret, resentment, and bitterness is not the truth of who we are. To resign ourselves to a life lived in subservience to these false laws of limitation and conflict is the ultimate and only sin- the denial of our inherent divinity.

Every human being is capable of unimaginable greatness. As a species imbued with the power of the divine, our belief of a thing makes it true. We are sovereign creators. If we believe it is possible to live a life of eternal inner peace, we can. If we believe it is possible to heal and restore the Earth, we can. Nothing is impossible to beings as great and good and powerful as humanity- the humanity that is *us*.

In this time of the Great Change, we will shake off the trappings of doubt as a dog may shake water from its coat. We will penetrate the assumptions that run our lives and dissolve them as easily as smoke on a breeze. We can create a world without fear, a world without suffering. We can create a world of magic and miracles far beyond the understanding of the mind. Our nature is unlimited, unbound, unfettered.

The Great Change is the time of converging prophesies when we step beyond the seeming apocalypse of our world and into the blossom of our apotheosis. In this movement from terror to knowing we finally claim the full power of our humanity. We discover that we have been God all along.

As we gather our divinity into our arms, we create a new world, one that honors and reveres all things as holy. In this new world, "human" is synonymous, not with weakness, but with boundlessness, with love, with power and with grace. "Human" is synonymous with God.

It is true that the world we have known is being shaken to its core. It shakes to wake us up. It shakes to loosen our hold on the entrenched illusion of reality that has clouded our vision.

Beyond, there is a garden awaiting us. It sits on the other side of fear and beckons us toward majesty. We will find the gateway to this Eden within, at the threshold of our own beating heart.

Leadership in the New Eden

I define the Great Change as the lifting of humanity into a new realm of consciousness. This is the consciousness of the heart, which abides in a continual state of natural and effortless harmony with all that is.

Humans are being released, once and for all, from all that is not in accord with love. That which is being shed includes fear, exploitation, cruelty, brutality, manipulation, and a reliance on the phenomenal world as our only reality. As this happens, we become lighter. We feel and accept all that is within us. We enter a world of transparency, miracles, and interconnectedness where we know once and for all that the life within us is the same that runs through all that is.

This is the shift to realizing the inner Eden. In the realm of the heart, we become both a part and the entirety of a living, breathing, differentiated whole that moves in seamless accord with divine will. While the shift from mind to heart may come upon us gently, it will be nevertheless absolute and irreversible. Those of us awakening now presage a complete transformation of our most fundamental ways of being as individuals, as a collective, as a species, and as a planet.

It is important to understand that this Great Change is happening whether we want it to or not. It is out of our control. The forces of evolution do not stop or slow according to our fears or preferences. However, the shift we are experiencing does not need to be full of suffering or fear.

The passage into this next phase of evolution will be eased when led by wayshowers who have allowed Eden to fully flourish within themselves. These are people who are willing to shine so brightly, so exuberantly, that they cannot help but show others the path forward. These leaders have surrendered their self-interest, their small self, and their fear of death to emerge as ones who demonstrate, by their very presence, a world of freedom that exists just beyond the known. These "leaders" have not necessarily set out to become leaders or wayshowers or guides or sages. They have simply followed the voice of their heart to realize their highest, most fulfilled expression. In so doing, they inspire others naturally and effortlessly to do the same.

Awareness, (or, the extent to which one knows and loves oneself) will be the "currency" of the coming era. Awareness cannot be faked, bought, manipulated, or achieved in the accepted sense of the word. It is developed only through a willingness to both love and surrender all that is.

As we step into awareness, we will no longer be prone to manipulation. We will no longer be drawn to empty rhetoric. We will hone our intuitive ability to parse out and dismiss offhand even the subtlest of lies. Therefore, those stepping forward into "power" and "positions of influence," those whom we will turn to in these coming times will be the ones who have awakened into their deepest authenticity. Those who have committed to awakening emit an unmistakable frequency. They will naturally and unselfconsciously spread empowerment and truth, and they will be instantly recognizable to others who have chosen the same path. This is how the voice of unity, power, and compassion will spread over the planet. It will be through the pulse, the vibration, the unerring draw toward that which is good, nourishing, and true.

Because the process of creation happens from the inside out, this book does not seek to fix, change, advise, or offer large-scale solutions to the systems that currently govern our world. Indeed, these systems cannot be "fixed," as they are not broken. They are simply founded upon (and therefore perpetuate) old models of consciousness. Creation is a free-will act that originates from within. As such, every manifested thing cannot help but reflect and perpetuate the level of consciousness of its creator. The systems we live within reflect the old level of consciousness of our species- the levels we are currently in the process of transcending.

The effort, then, the discipline and devotion that is asked of emerging leaders is not to run themselves into exhaustion resisting and "fixing" the external world of form, but to take full responsibility for- and command of- the internal world from which the external emanates. In this way, the leaders in these coming times will be those who have first realized Eden within their own being.

It is indeed a delightful irony that in order to live in harmonious community we must first plumb the depths of our own individuality. This momentous decision to turn inward may be accompanied by a cacophony of voices (your own and others) defaming you for what looks like defection from the world. It is a great declaration of worthiness to continue turning inward in the face of all that contrives to pull you from your path.

Creating a thriving life is both your joy and sovereign responsibility. It happens through the accumulation of choices you make that resonate with your deepest needs and most natural way of being. Again and again this book offers confirmation that your commitment to self-study and the elevation of your own consciousness is by far the most important decision of your life.

As you come to know the depths of your human experience, as you reclaim forgotten aspects of self, and re-assemble (or, re-member) yourself into wholeness, you will eventually discover something very wonderful. One day you will look up and see the healing you allowed for yourself reflected in the world around you. You begin, effortlessly, to transmit healing and love to all who cross your path. You see that your inner devotion created a wellspring of love and peace that could not help but flow into the world.

Finally, you will understand that all this time, when you thought you were taking care of yourself and learning the lessons you needed to learn, you were actually serving all of humanity. This is because you are not separate from creation. All of the universe resides already within you. Therefore, when you love yourself, you love all. It is that simple.

Awakening from Prison

"Why, when God's world is so big, did you fall asleep in a prison of all places?"
-Rumi

All over the world humans are waking up. The tectonic shaking of the world is calling us to open our eyes, and as we "come to" from what has amounted to a long nightmare, the surroundings we behold upon awakening happen to be the four, stark walls of an illusory- though extremely compelling- prison.

Many have awakened enough to see that they are living in a prison of sorts, but most do not know how to get out of it. There are many brash and flashing lights offering false and interminable paths through the prison's endless labyrinth. What is the true light and how can we orient ourselves toward it? How can we distinguish between the light of the soul and the misleading (but seductive) light of the ego? Centuries of deep sleep, of dogged routine, of addictions, of enduring and perpetrating shock, shame, and trauma, have veiled the way out of the darkness.

When opening the eyes to a situation such as this it can be very, very tempting to panic.

In this way this moment of collective awakening, so long anticipated, is also a delicate and vital time on our planet. All of humanity, in its innocent stirring from slumber, could very easily lose their heads at surroundings they find themselves in.

This is what makes true leadership so necessary at this time. Those of us who have found a way out of prison and into the "world so big" that Rumi describes can and indeed *must* stand up now. Those of us who have penetrated the darkness of our fears, who have followed the subtle beckoning of our soul, know that all is possible, nothing is beyond redemption, and anything can be restored. This understanding is the piercing, unmistakable light of grace that penetrates the darkness of prison where so many are trapped.

The wisdom encoded in this book has emerged from my own commitment to turn again and again toward the loving, gentle, and all-encompassing light of grace. This is the light that casts no shadow. It is a state of being that has no opposite. This book offers light like waves breaking against a shore. Every word, every statement is simply a new wave emerging from the same ocean, a susurration of peace and truth that calls you again and again toward your greatness.

This book is designed to help you find that light within yourself. It is a translation of spirit through the ancient mechanism of the Word, offering a divine technology that resides as a bridge between the unknown and the manifested. It is a drawing of spirit into the earliest stages of form- that is, belief.

This book transmits the unmistakable frequency of the heart- the frequency that will lead each of us safely through the delicate process of transitioning out of an ego-dominated reality. This book offers the time and space for you to recognize clearly the voice and frequency of your own divine heart. As you do so you will see the way of your own apotheosis unfolding before you.

The Role of the Heart

The New Eden is whispering her secrets for those willing to hear them. These secrets are simultaneously ancient and unprecedented, at once true and unpredictable. As we seek the path to our own apotheosis, we hear that there is only one compass that can take us safely over the threshold and into the terrain beyond. That is, of course, the voice of our heart.

The heart, as we will explore further, is a vastly misunderstood - and often denigrated- instrument. Far from being merely "warm and fuzzy" (some insipid thing to be trotted out on Valentine's Day for dutiful homage) the heart is, in truth, the most powerful aspect of self. Our human heart is a hologram of the sacred heart of the universe. As such, it offers capacity for unlimited creation, unconditional healing, and miraculous restoration of all that is good, worthy, and sacred. This is true, not "in theory," but practically, visibly, and measurably in our lives.

The heart can, and does, manifest miracles in the physical realm. With the heart as our instrument of creation, we effortlessly bring our will into being without fear of reprisal or negative influence, without needing to apply for "permission" from outside sources or systems, and without having to apologize for it, atone for it, earn it, or prove ourselves worthy. The incredible power of the heart is the unconditional birthright of our humanity, and it has already been granted.

Despite its universal presence, the heart's power is largely untapped. It cannot be accessed by the mind nor used for personal gain at the expense of others. Therefore, it is a living secret in our world, as it can only be accessed and utilized by one who has surrendered their ego. Such a surrendered person acts effortlessly in concert with the totality of all that is, which means their choices and creations cannot help but benefit all beings.

The heart is a place of stillness, of surrender, of inner peace. It tells us that gentleness is the most powerful force in the Universe. However, though the heart is yin, it is by no means *passive*. It is not rationally linear, and yet it is undeniably practical. The heart operates by a higher logic that rejects nothing, encompasses all, is complete, and whole and yet always moving toward resolution.

The New Eden will be realized through the heart. This state of being dawns when we allow ourselves to be our most natural, most effortless, most joyful version of self. This self is very different from the one we *think* we are. The Edenic self is the higher self, the true self that moves always in accordance with our internal rhythms.

We talk much of ego death. There is a pervasive belief that to turn from the ego and toward the heart must necessarily be a painful enterprise, full of will-power, discipline, and the dogged conquering of fears. However, the belief that life, change, and spiritual transformation needs to be difficult is simply another pervasive campaign of the ego. In contrast, this book offers a gentle and even enjoyable pedagogy of transformation.

Eden will dawn simply. Peace comes through the practice of peace. The path to gentleness is to simply be gentle. The path to compassion is to practice compassion. In the Edenic state, there is no difference between *having* and *being,* and none whatsoever between *doing* and *being*. In the coming era, we will merge this trinity of "having," "doing," and "being" into one.

In the same way that peace comes about through practicing peace, the New Eden will be realized in a way that is reflective of its very nature- that is, through the practice of tenderness, love, compassion, and truth. The practice for us, who are so accustomed to dramatic suffering, rigorous initiations, and the extremes of existence, will be to trust that our transformation is no less profound for being subtle and full of joy.

I have listened to my own heart, turning toward it again and again against all "logic," and this book is my offering of the knowledge that emerged from that practice. This book shines with the wisdom that brought me through my own awakening and through my times of deepest darkness. It offers the movement beyond faith into knowing, standing as a testimony to the ways in which I have been supported, held, and led to safety against all of the odds purported by the harsh and clamoring world. This book holds the truths that brought me back into life and into my own inner Eden. It is a map of the path I trod again and again back to the sanctuary of my heart. I can offer nothing more and nothing less than that.

Intentions and Roadmap for this Book

The heart, while often talked about, is not easy to access in a culture that prioritizes empirical rationality as the only acceptable way to understand the world. Many people don't actually know the difference between the head and the heart. They think they have accessed their hearts because they can describe it, or because they know the right words to say. I promise you, the heart cannot be accessed through thinking about it.

Many of us have spent years barricading ourselves from our own hearts. It is, after all, a terrifying thing, the heart. It cares nothing for our preconceptions, our nicely ordered reality, our opinions on how the world "should" work. It is wild, unpredictable, and impossible to control. It cannot be demanded of, nor pleaded with, and it absolutely cannot be accessed by force. Instead, it must be approached like the wild thing it is- with reverence, humility, and absolute authenticity. When we come into accord with the heart, we will know. But how do we come to it? How do we discern its quiet voice, its gentle light, from the relentless noise and brash searchlight of our thinking mind?

I have learned that it does no good to deny the head and its need for empirical rationality. The hungry mind must be met in its need for thought. As the mind is met, it relaxes into trust. As it does so, its immense power can be harnessed in service to divine creation.

So, to accommodate these aspects of the self – the rational mind and creative heart- this book is laid out in two parts. It offers a journey from head to heart, which provides a pathway for unifying (and thus transcending) the two. In this way, the book leads us gently away from the mind without needing to do battle with it. We can loosen our dependence on thought, access the intelligence of our heart, and ultimately bring into harmony these two immense, wondrous, and co-creative aspects of self.

Summary of Part I: Teachings of the New Eden

Part I engages the thinking mind with the intention of moving it into expansion and openness. Here I examine familiar and influential archetypes through the lens of the higher mind. These underlying concepts and our interpretation of them are currently hidden from view, assumed to be true and sacrosanct and thus shoved out of sight into the deepest parts of our collective subconscious. While hidden, they nevertheless form the foundation of our current (hellish) collective reality. These concepts include assumptions of sin, debt, the inevitability of suffering, and the unquestionably fallen state of humanity (perpetuated by our retelling of story of Adam and Eve).

In Part I, I dredge up these concepts from where they reside in the depths of our subconscious and expose them through the safe light of the loving heart. This uncovering opens the door for us to retell the entire story of our humanity through the lens of unconditional love and compassion. As the mind is presented with new ways of conceiving of old ideas, it becomes limber and supple in its willingness approach the world anew.

Chapter 1

In Chapter One I invoke the ancient healing process of Reversing to re-examine the birth of humanity through the lens of unconditional love. In doing so, I retell the story of humanity's origin- the story of Adam and Eve. Through the eye of the heart, we reframe Eve as a necessary and archetypal force of evolution instead of a figure to be reviled, judged, and vilified. We see how her symbolic decision to eat the apple launched humanity into the heroic evolutionary journey which we are currently resolving: that is, the journey of our own conscious apotheosis.

In this first chapter I show that all of humanity stands at the threshold of a New Eden. This forthcoming Eden is the legacy seeded by Eve- it is her promise and her gift to us. It is, as mentioned earlier, the irreversible transition from head to heart- from evolving merely to survive to evolving to thrive. I discuss what thriving really is (hint: it's not a thoughtform), and I provide points of contemplation for making that shift now, in practical and measurable ways, in your own life.

Chapter 2

The second chapter offers a series of contemplations that emerged from my lived experiences as I sought to make sense of the world after my own awakening. The three years in which this book was incubated saw me wrestling with the questions that arose after my experiences of death, darkness, loss, and betrayal. These questions did not let me rest until I had found stability by touching again and again on the immutable divine law that abides at the bedrock of creation.

In these contemplations I draw from the wisdom of that repeated journey through the underworld of my own fears. I peer through the lens of the higher mind to examine such concepts as original sin, redemption, money and debt, atonement, unconditional love, the conflict between men and women, the nature of embodiment, and the power of the heart to manifest miracles.

Summary of Part II: Visualizations for Embodying the New Eden

In Part Two we let the limbered mind subside into its natural state of expansion and turn toward the door of the heart. This second part consists of eight visualizations that emerged from the ancient healing modality known as Heart Imagery. Heart Imagery is a powerful, interdimensional method of accessing the heart while allowing the thinking mind to rest in openness and trust. It is similar to modalities such as shamanic journeying, lucid dreaming, and quantum hypnosis.

This part of the book offers the opportunity for accelerated transformation. These visualizations were knit together from the visons, images, and revelations that came to me as I sought my own path to healing. The journeys penetrate deep into the archetypal realm that governs our reality, allowing us to re-frame our own stories, hear the voice of our higher self, and deepen our trust in the larger powers at our command. Through these visualizations we can dramatically enhance our powers of self-possession and conscious alignment with our truth. These visualizations exist outside of linear time, and thus offer the miracle of instant healing.

The first visualization, "Conscious Rebirth," is an introduction to the modality of Heart Imagery. It sets the container for the rest of the journey, creating a space of protection, safety, and relaxation.

The remaining seven visualizations correspond to the seven traits that I developed through the years in which this book was incubated. I developed these traits instinctively without knowing what I was doing. It was only in retrospect that I was able to classify them as a framework.

These traits helped me to trust a reality beyond the one I knew with my rational brain. They gave me the strength and confidence to live in, and manifest, a world parallel to the hellish and resigned reality in which so much of humanity resides. Through embodying these traits, I learned to re-engage with the world without fear of "losing" the higher reality that I had accessed.

Each trait is accorded its own visualization and is accompanied by a short teaching. The visualizations emerged from the universal sacred heart and are woven from the visions, images, and inner-plane experiences that continuously stabilized my own awakening in the three years that I wrote this book.

The traits and corresponding visualizations are as follows:

Chapter 3: Purpose

How to determine your deepest purpose and access your highest divine gifts.

Chapter 4: Integrity

How to align and empower your whole being with the truth of your heart.

Chapter 5: Emptiness

How to become comfortable with the vast expanse of nothing and create from the infinite space of the heart.

Chapter 6: Presence

How to listen deeply, surrender doubt, and manifest from a place of stillness and confidence in your indomitable divine will.

Chapter 7: Trust

How to confront fear without fear. How to release all that is heavy.

Chapter 8: Sovereignty

How to rule your inner king/queendom with grace and empowerment.

Chapter 9: Devotion

How to worship- and become- the divinity that you already are.

The teachings and visualizations in this book usher the essence of the New Eden into your body, anchoring it as an unquestioned knowing within your conscious mind. The journeys will be experienced differently by every person, providing an opportunity for you to develop a highly-individualized understanding of your own personal evolution.

How to Read this Book

The Visualizations

For your first time reading this book I strongly suggest that you work with the visualizations in order, taking time between each one for integration, contemplation, and reflection. The visualizations carry an intelligence, rhythm, and intuitive curriculum of their own. Your higher self will guide you through the visualizations at the right pace.

Once you have journeyed through all visualizations in order and taken time to integrate, feel free to go back and listen or read at any time in any order.

There are also recordings available if you would prefer to have the container held for you.[1]

Preparing for Change

This book has tremendous power to awaken change in you. The changes may be subtle, even unrecognizable at first. They will occur in the deepest realms of your subconscious, re-forming you from your foundation up. While profound, the shifts are designed to be gentle, natural, and effortless.

They will, however, require surrender, and they will most likely require tending. Take time to listen, to meet yourself, to move through the processes asked of you by your higher self. Trust that your body and soul will guide you to stabilize the transformations you are experiencing.

It is vital at this time to allow yourself to gravitate toward that which supports you. It is not weakness or denial of spirit move away from that which cannot meet you. As you anchor the frequencies of the New Eden into your body, let yourself be gentle, loving, and responsive to your needs. Seek out the people, places, environments, and lifestyles that feel nourishing to you. Do not be afraid to say "no" to that which cannot hold you. You can choose what, and whom, you allow entry to the sacred temple of your life. Without apology or explanation, let your body, instinct, intuition, and inner guiding system turn you toward your most natural, nourishing, and fulfilling way of being. These internal sources of wisdom are taking you toward your birthright of peace.

---

[1] You can find these recordings at www.booksofeden.com

A Note on Terminology

The Divine

In this book I invoke a higher plane of existence, which I refer to as "the divine." This is the part of self that exists, unchanging, beyond the world of form. In invoking the divine, I espouse no religion, scripture, dogma, or single wisdom tradition. I believe this higher power (which I refer to interchangeably as source, God, the divine, the universe, the Mother, Spirit, the heart, and life force) needs no specific conduit to come to Earth. It is simply present wherever there is love.

The New Eden

This book is founded on the premise that humanity stands poised to step over an unprecedented threshold of evolution. On one side is the illusory, mind-dominated reality and on the other is the field of the divine heart. I refer to the moment of stepping over the threshold as both The Great Change and The Apotheosis, and I refer interchangeably to the next phase of evolution as the New Earth, the New Eden, and the new era of consciousness. Each of these means, simply, a world beyond conflict in which all beings thrive into their fullest, most natural expression.

I refer to this collective state of thriving as: unity consciousness, oneness consciousness, and Christ consciousness interchangeably. All of these terms refer simply to one thing: a loving recognition of the interconnectedness of all things.

The Stories of Humanity

You will notice I refer to many concepts that have been long regarded as exclusive territory of the church, temple, and synagogue. I make no apology for engaging with the ideas and structures of religion, as it is the stories and traditions of these religions that have so greatly influenced our Western culture. Concepts such as original sin, redemption, forgiveness, atonement, and debt carry very specific connotations that, whether or not we have ever set foot in a religious institution, greatly affect our deepest, most hidden subconscious, and therefore form the basis of our daily reality.

I honor the fact that many of the terms I use- such as "sin," "atonement," and "debt," to name a few- come steeped in tradition and can mean many different things to different people. Within this book, these terms serve a very particular purpose. I define them precisely, and I use them precisely, in ways that are most likely new and unfamiliar. In allowing yourself to let go of preconceptions, these terms can come to life in a way that brings healing and release.

I draw stories and teachings from many different wisdom traditions, including Christianity, Hinduism, and the Kabbalah. However, my references are not influenced by the dogma of organized religion. I believe that the stories of these traditions are encoded with ancient memories and secrets that live hidden within the text. As such, these stories are invaluable for illuminating ideas and teachings that are deeply, recursively human.

Though practical and earthly, this book also holds spiritual and mystical transmissions. What I mean to emphasize throughout, though, is that the divine is not some remote and far-away thing. It is an ever-present force that dwells in the humblest moments of our daily reality. It lives in the smallest, the simplest, the quietest of places, and it goes by many, many names. When I invoke the heart, spirit, soul, and higher self, I refer to that clear, in-dwelling, and eternally-loving voice that guides us when our mind is quiet. The divine is not esoteric and remote, but simple, natural, and always present. It is the deepest truth of our nature.

With that, let us begin.

Part I: Teachings of the New Eden

Chapter 1: Eden

Like the ouroboros,[2] we will begin at the end, and end at the beginning. That is, with Eden.

Eden is not theoretical. It is not an ethereal dream, nor is it a myth. It is a real place. Moreover, it is not, nor has it ever been, lost. It has only been forgotten.

Eden is the highest expression of your being. It manifests the moment that you begin to live your most natural life. This is a life of thriving, governed by joy and peace, a life of wholeness, when you embrace as a gift your unassailable freedom.

In order to live your highest expression, you must begin with the assumption that nothing about you is flawed. There aren't any "extra parts" to your being. When you were created, it was with impeccable intention. The parts about yourself that you would change (or that others wish you would change)- those attributes you would call "imperfections," are actually portals through which you will realize your fullest potential. When every aspect of your body, mind, and soul is brought into the light of compassion, reverence, and self-love, you see the divine mind at work. You understand how perfectly you were created to fulfill the purpose for which you were born.

In order to live in this way, you must know who you truly are. You do this by listening, watching, and holding yourself in every moment without judgment or blame. As you do this, you become open to receiving the deep truth of your nature. This unreserved reception of self is a radical act of courage. You fear that when you open the locked doors of your being, you will see that which is dark, shameful, cruel. Instead, you will find, over and over again, that the root of all you are is only love.

---

[2] It is not lost on me that the ouroboros is a serpent! A very potent image given our subject matter.

Underneath the voices you've absorbed, the messages you've integrated, the stories you've learned, thrums a living template of truth. This truth speaks through the rhythms of your body, the blood in your living network of veins, the longings of your heart. This inner truth is undeniable, pure, and unchanging. It is the love and peace from which you were created and into which you return. This abiding truth is your very own inviolable sanctuary, your in-dwelling Garden of Eden, and you stand even now at its gates.

To enter, you must come to know yourself anew- beyond judgement and shame, beyond stories, beyond what you've been told about yourself and "how-the-world-works." As you peel back the layers that have for so long obscured your authentic expression, you will invariably find that you no longer "fit" into the world as you know it. The only option, then, is to create a new world- one in which you are as limitless, as expansive, as free as you know yourself to be in truth.

The Living Memory of Eden

The garden is our guiding archetype for the New Eden. It has much to teach us about flourishing, thriving, and the nature of harmonic creation.

When we consider a garden, we see that every plant, every flower, is encouraged to bloom into its own fullest expression. The thriving garden is tended in such a way that each individual shoot is given all it needs to prosper. Taken together, the garden is a community of perfect fluorescence. It is abundance and generosity; it freely offers nourishment for all of our senses: herbs and flowers, fruit and living food. Tumbling and brimming with life, the garden is manifested hope, a model for body, life, and the complex ecosystem of humanity on Earth.

The garden invites us to breathe deeply as it offers manifest order and harmony, balance, and intention. The orderly aspect of a garden comes about through continual care- not through the hard labor of plow and till, but through the gentler devotion of hand and hoe. With this intimate tending, the garden thrives. A touch here, a touch there allows it to burst to life in free and wild joy, held in the loving constructs that contain and direct its beauty.

As our guiding archetype for the new era of consciousness, the garden has much to show us. One of its primary teachings is the way it holds the synergistic balance of the holy trinity- the Mother, Father, and Child- which is the governing principle of creation on Earth. The garden offers a living model for the harmonious interdependence of these energies, demonstrating how Mother (feminine), Father (masculine), and Child (neutral) work together, not through conflict and competition, but through loving and surrendered devotion.

The garden beds are tended with precision, care, discernment, and intention (the masculine aspect) in such a way that the boundless life within them (the feminine aspect) can flourish. Within and around the flowers, plants and buds is the neutral, empty space, the limitless and ever-present void that beckons the expansion of life. This latter aspect is both masculine and feminine, or, neither. It is the child, the neutral element, the aspect of the trinity that invites evolution and growth.

In this way, the paradox presented by the ouroboros lives within the garden itself, revealing a great truth about the power that drives our evolution. It is in actuality the child- the neutral aspect of the holy trinity- that came first. The neutral space is what allows for the masculine and feminine energies to express fully. The creative tension, the unsolvable nature of in this paradox (that the child's formless will is the force that brought the mother and father into being, and not the other way around) ensures that life itself will never end. In this way, we evolve into greater and greater expressions of sophistication in an attempt to "catch up" to the playful, unbound desire of the child, from whom the motivation for all life emanates.

This understanding of evolution bends time. We see we are in actuality moving forward in a template that was created *backwards,* with the ending as first thing brought into existence. It is as though the denouement of the book is already written, and all else moves toward that inevitable conclusion. The ending may resolve itself through conflict and unpredictable plot twists, but the ending is already safely inscribed in the annals of time. It ensures that we move always and inexorably toward grace. [3]

In the same way that it was the unborn child that assured the life of its parents (and so on and so on back to the beginning of time), Eden as well exists as a memory within us. It is, however, a memory of the future. Eden lives within each of us in the same way that a flower lives as a memory imprinted within a seed. It is undeniable, unassailable, and irresistible. It beckons us ever onwards toward the harmonic Earth that we know exists.

There is no point, then, in looking with nostalgia on times long past, because Eden lives within us as our future state. It is imprinted on our being as a template of harmony that, because it feels so very *real*, it is mistaken as a memory of a past era. Eden hums underneath the veils of our illusory world like a river rushing beneath ice. We *know* it is there. It is the very force of our evolution, the desire beneath all desires. It is as real and inevitable as the final expression of the flower within a seed.

---

[3] This is not, as it may seem at first an impingement on free will. As we expand in consciousness we tap into the vast and timeless aspect of self that wrote the ending in the first place.

The Personal and the Collective Eden

This book brings with it a promise. The world at large, and many we meet, may seem very far from living in the promise of peace and harmony, love, and transparency. It is, however, possible to manifest this Eden within your body and life within this lifetime. It is possible to anchor this Eden in your body, cells, and subconscious so that peace, relaxation, and goodwill is your default state of being. What's more, the process of realizing your inner Eden is perhaps much quicker, more gentle, more natural, and much more enjoyable than you may believe in the moment.

In witnessing the gap between the truth of our nature and the world at large, it is tempting to rush out, brandishing our swords of truth and trying to force all we meet to bend into accordance with the peace and harmony we feel is possible. However, it is vital to understand that Eden must first dawn within the self. Before rallying to change the world, each of us must first bring Eden to life in our own way- in our bodies and in our lives. This intimate journey of self-discovery lets us understand the process, the wisdom, the strength, and courage that is needed on this path. As we do this our very being, our very presence shows the way forward for others. When we live unencumbered by fear, our very lives stand as effortless testimonies of what was once considered impossible. Others will be drawn to our blooming radiance, seeking their own empowerment within the world's rigid- and ultimately fragile- declaration of darkness. As those we meet catch the scent of hope, they follow the path to their own awakening. In this way, one by one we will burst into bloom across the planet, and spring will come to Earth at last.

Awakening to Power

A garden flourishes in its own time. We cannot rush our manifestation of self nor force the Eden that is templated within us to blossom according to our personal preferences. Yet there does exist a direct path to its realization. I speak of the open and surrendered way of the heart.

The path of the heart is joyful and natural, but it also requires immense courage. We are, after all, human. We were designed to live on this planet, to feel and love and harness the extremes of human existence. Our heart and bodies know how to do this. But the opening, the bursting into blossom, will also bring us in full contact with our suffering.

We will find, as we strip away the ice from the rushing river of our lives, that there suddenly exist no barriers between ourselves and the world. In the same way that blood flows back into a frozen limb, this sudden influx of life-force can be very intense, especially at first. As we grow larger than the small and fragile barriers of our fears, our ability to *feel* is equally amplified. We feel our own pain and suffering acutely even as we feel our own immense capacity for love, connection, and joy.

The love that we open to can be terrifying because it engulfs us with the force of a tidal wave, washing away all that is small, petty, and constricted. As flash floods carve into the living earth vast desert canyons, the immense love we open to cleaves new channels into our very being. We emerge from the experience changed- fearless and unbound in our capacity to feel.

It does, however, take some time to adjust to this new way of being. When I experienced my awakening, it felt as though the layers of callous I had built up to interact with the world had dissolved. My whole being felt as raw and exposed as the skin beneath a torn fingernail. The world around me, even those whom I loved dearly, became, for a time, impossible to connect with. Anything but the utmost tenderness could not be borne.

As a result, I retreated for as long as was necessary to nourish myself and stabilize this new way of being. The final year of this retreat was one of almost unbroken solitude. In that time, I gained strength. I understood that I could not yet rely on the outside world to be my Eden, so I would need to learn to carry it within myself as a living sanctuary.

Through those long months of inner listening, I learned to distinguish between the clear, loving, empowering voice of my heart and "everything else." The "everything else" were the layers of conditioning that stood as barriers to my inner sanctuary. Over time, the voice of my heart became stronger, clearer, and more real than the clamoring voice of the world. In this way I learned, not to retreat from the world, but to engage with it- not from a place of resistance, anger, or judgment, but from a place of acceptance, compassion, and truth.

So, in the process of awakening, we take the time we need to heal, to adjust, to grow stronger, to tend to the small and fragile shoots of our new garden, but ultimately, we must know that we will be called back into service of this world that we love so much. Our gifts will inevitably bring us outside of our own smallness, guiding us into a place of active engagement, and showing us how to give ourselves freely, fearlessly, and unselfconsciously from a place of worthiness and self-love. These gifts, when we give them, will reveal us, and they will reveal to others a world far, far different and more beautiful than we could imagine.

The way of the heart offers transparency. After the courageous and vulnerable revelation of self, we will experience the invulnerability, the invincibility, and the empowerment that comes with having nothing whatsoever to hide. Radiating our inner light, all that we face up to within ourselves even that which seemed intractable, will wither away, revealing something breathtaking underneath.

We have turned away from the Earth's suffering because we have felt helpless in the face of it. But we are not helpless. As the limitless, creative power of our heart surfaces into our waking consciousness, we discover that our very love has the power to command miracles. When we wake up to this truth, untold wonder abounds in our lives.

I do not mean this figuratively. Though it works mysteriously, the divine is, above all things, practical. Our love and devotion will always lead to the manifestation of literal, visible, measurable, and empirical miracles that transform and restore our physical world. These miracles may be astonishing, like a butterfly emerging from a cocoon, or they may be simple and, to anyone else, unremarkable. But once we attune to the divine at work in our lives, we will see over and over again its loving hand, guiding, intervening, and creating joyful and unexpected paths towards our fulfillment.

We are afraid to truly look at ourselves and our world because we fear it is too late for redemption. But I tell you truly: it is never too late. Nothing is impossible, and nothing is out of reach of divine will. The divine does not work on a linear timeline; it is not restricted to what seems logical or rational. The power of belief, of forgiveness and heartfelt intention can wipe out centuries of destruction within a matter of weeks, of days. Of moments. The loving intention of our faith creates wormholes within the mutable fabric of time. As each of us claims our own worthiness to live simply and in joy, the world falls, naturally, into pace with divine will. It is possible for us to restore all to harmony, balance, and naturalness.

As we shake off numbness and apathy and open to the immense experience of this human life, we will move through chaos and into peace. We will touch suffering and then step beyond it. Our heart speaks to us through joy and harmony, through words of comfort and empowerment that lead us beyond duality. We no longer need to embrace asceticism, suffering, or self-denial as paths to enlightenment. We do not need to know misery in order to know happiness, or to experience goodness only in contrast to darkness and fear. We can experience our joy now as a pure state, one with no opposite that exists already whole and complete. As we do so, we release the need for comparison- we see that duality is no longer a necessary mechanism for growth.

When we follow joy, tenderness, and self-love, Eden unfolds simply. Joy is the voice of the heart that will lead us to realize our highest, most exuberant blossoming. This joy emanates from the very center of our being, guiding us along the thread of our heart's deepest longings, taking us on an adventurous journey to our inevitable fulfillment.

This is the joy of the flower opening into bloom. It is your most natural and effortless expression of self. As you learn to give your deepest gifts, the transparency of self will become evident in your offerings. The full transmission of your natural being becomes visible in each movement you make. Your past, every moment of pain and joy and growth, all of the wisdom you've earned, will be gathered into your heart and offered as a gift. This gift, your unique genius, will hold the unmistakable frequency of your soul. This is the highest form alchemy- transmuting your very life into the gift that heals the world. This is the path and the power of the heart. Through it you become a living prayer-a walking embodiment of the eternal Eden.

"And the Fruit"

Of Man's First Disobedience, and the Fruit
Of that Forbidden Tree...

-John Milton, Paradise Lost

We have been speaking of Eden. We know now that it does not belong to some far-off time. We know it isn't a paradise long lost or a fixed place somewhere on Earth that must be endlessly sought. We know now that the New Eden refers to the in-dwelling state of peace and love accessible through the heart of each human being. We know that, as a collective, we stand at the threshold of this divine garden.

To anchor these understandings we will now plunge into the mythic history of Eden. It is time, once and for all, to unwrap the layers of illusion that prevent us from receiving our divine birthright of perfect sovereignty. It is time to dissolve the unconscious, deeply hidden resistance to entering our awaiting garden of peace. It is time to retell the story of humanity's origin through the eyes of a God who looks upon all, not with judgment and wroth, but with unconditional love. We will begin with our original progenitors, Adam and Eve. They have much to teach us.

Re-writing the Story of Humanity

For much of the Western world, the creation story of humanity refers to a moment in time when Eve ate of the fruit of the Tree of Knowledge. We know this story well. Eve ate and offered the fruit to Adam, who also ate. They then realized they were naked and felt shame. They sewed fig leaves together to cover themselves, and they hid in the bushes. They were discovered and cast out of Eden by a wrathful God, cursed to endure pain, sorrow, and death.

We have spent many eons castigating Eve for her duplicity and Adam for the abhorrent weakness of his trust. With this story we have tainted the labor of motherhood with the brush of shame and condemnation. And Adam, with his labor in the fields- we have damned him to the joyless drudgery of survival. Unable to see the larger context of this fateful decision, humanity fell into conflict and reprisal, engaging in an ongoing battle of the sexes that has been exhaustively played out over the centuries by hurt, traumatized, oppressed, and suppressed men and women.

This punitive reading of the story of our antecedents can no longer carry us forward. It has no place in the new era that is upon us. It is time to retell the story of humanity's birth.

To retell, however, we must first let go of the old, tired narrative that rules us. Release and surrender is the ultimate pathway to our apotheosis, however, it is rarely as easy as "just letting go." To let go, we often need to hear the words, or receive a specific understanding that unlocks our hearts and unclenches our hands. The path of ascension can be seen as a journey to gather these keys of truth so that we may be unlocked and released. The keys will show us the mysterious and hidden "why" behind our fears, proclivities, and actions. They lift us from a place of condemnation into the realm of compassionate understanding. These keys give us an "of course!" moment where we finally understand *why* we are the way we are.

The keys for unlocking the self dwell within each and every person. They will be found, not in the mind, but in the mysterious realm of the subconscious. We can access this realm in many ways. In this book, I invoke the method that worked for me, that is, the ancient and mystical healing modality known as "Reversing" (which is closely connected to the healing modality of Heart Imagery used in the second half of this book). These methods are connected in that each they plunge us into the powerful realm of the image, the archetype, and the ancient memories of the soul that live dormant and waiting within us.

Reversing offers the opportunity to indelibly rewrite our past through the heart's lens of unconditional love. To do this, however, we must experience our past, not through the veil of the mind and memory, but immediately and viscerally. The entire journey of our soul is recorded in our heart as images, feelings, and memories- not as thoughtforms.

Through the modalities of Reversing and Heart Imagery, we go back in time to consciously and lovingly touch on the painful memories that imprinted trauma and separation into our psyche. In accessing these memories, we are better able understand who we are, why we behave the way we do, and what is our purpose in this lifetime. As these memories surface, we see ourselves suddenly as innocent beings who have been placed in a much larger, more complex context that we could ever comprehend with our thinking mind. This releases the pressure of self-judgement as we see that our triggers, fears, and reactions are not "our fault," but the natural result of past experiences and traumas that have been imprinted onto us over time. The ultimate goal of Reversing is not to excuse or justify our behavior, but to guide us into an expanded plane of consciousness where we can access the multi-dimensional and complex drivers that lay behind our every decision. This generates a wider lens of understanding so that our triggers, fears, and reactions decouple from shame and thus dissolve automatically in the light of awareness.

Reversing allows us to drill down to the bedrock of our existence in order to authentically retell the stories of our lives- not as another layered thoughtform, but as the true story, the only story- the story of our unassailable innocence.

Humans are inveterate storytellers- it is the gift of living in a dimension that has been slowed and stretched into the miracle of linear time. The story is an exclusive privilege of our human experience as it can only come into being when there is a feeling of past, present, and future. The story is our gift and our birthright- it is the ethereal reflection of the Earth herself.

As humans, we are free to create any story at all and, given our free will, that story will automatically become true. The stories we tell and the stories we believe form our experience of the world. In the New Era, we are being given the opportunity to create stories of genuine harmony, love, and peace. However, to live in that way we must first unravel the subconscious influences that are currently preventing us from telling those stories authentically.

Given the very long history of suffering that humanity has lived through, we are primed to automatically interpret moments of shame, shock, and trauma as evidence of exploitation, abandonment, and as a statement on our unworthiness. These unconscious and inherited interpretations give rise to the stories of suffering that influence our entire lives. The seeds of these stories were often formed in childhood before we had learned to speak.

The healing modality of Reversing uses the underlying, wordless language of archetypes to penetrate the dense, accumulated layers of "reason" that we have formed over the top of our innocent moments of shame, shock, and trauma. A small child, without language to give it shape, experiences the devastation of shock as a feeling, perhaps as an image or a somatic impulse in the body. It is only later when faculties of reasoning are developed that the child uses language and thought patterns to build ever-more sophisticated stories that "explain" that first, crushing impact dealt by the world.

Because this first instance was not experienced through the mind, we cannot use the mind and its mechanisms- reason and language- to reach and heal the origin of our suffering. The child that experienced the shock, shame, or trauma receives the world through feminine modalities of sensory experience, images, and emotions.

Because the modality of Reversing uses images and archetypes- a universal, feminine, "right-brain" language of impression and frequency felt by the body itself- it speaks directly to the inner child, in the child's language. It pierces the heavy layers of words, justification, reasoning, and complex, crisscrossing, mind-created storylines and touches directly on the center of the trauma, shock, or shame that was the origin of all of these stories in the first place. Using the modality of Reversing, an adult human can go back in time and rewrite, *for good*, the stories that keep them trapped in cycles of abuse, failure, fear, and shame.

We hesitate to use Reversing in our lives because we fear this threshold of irreversible healing. We have come to believe that the stories we tell are the only things keeping us safe. It is important to understand, however, that when we rewrite the stories that determine our experience of the world, the knowledge we have gained from struggle or suffering is not lost or erased, only transmuted into higher awareness. In the process of Reversing, we do not lose our hard-earned wisdom; we are simply freed from the limiting beliefs of our own culpability. We are given access to the nameless origin of our suffering. As we do so, all is automatically forgiven. We finally see ourselves as blameless, and we claim the freedom to stop judging ourselves for all of the decisions we have made. We become, not a convict on trial for our crimes, but a defendant watching as all of the universe intervenes to proclaim our innocence.

All of life moves in fractal patterns, therefore it is possible to understand the trajectory of the whole human species from the journey of single human being. Just as one human may interpret childhood events as evidence of unworthiness or shame, we see, in the story of The Fall, an original, collective instance of shock, shame, and trauma that early humans interpreted as a betrayal of God. As all of the Universe abides in all things, we see that, if Reversing can completely heal the life of a single human, it will be equally effective in healing the collective trauma of humanity.

When humans were young and the consciousness of self-reference newly emerged into the world, something happened, a cataclysmic event that touched all of humanity.[4] The collective reacted as a child may do when experiencing shock for the first time, and this event became imprinted on the collective consciousness as evidence of unworthiness and separation from divinity. Later, in our increasing levels of sophistication and awareness, we created stories to justify this impression of separation. The story of Adam and Eve is one such story where we interpret events of the past through the lens of shame, judgment, unworthiness, punishment, and blame. The cataclysmic event, such as it was, was interpreted as evidence of being abandoned by God, which then took the form of a wordless imprint in the collective psyche of humanity. We have since spent eons living out that original imprinting, thus gathering more and more evidence as to its "truth."

It is, however, not the truth. Separation, abandonment, shame, inherent evil, and unworthiness is *not* the truth of who we are. It has simply been told, retold, and reinforced by centuries of misconception of the mind.

It is clear that we cannot use the thinking mind to undo the thicket of logic and reason that was built to make meaning of that first, calamitous experience of trauma. It was the mind that created the thicket in the first place! The closed mind is like a wood-chipper- anything you feed into it - from natural deadwood to a living, sacred oak tree- will be chewed up and spit out as identical grains of

---

[4] I am still investigating the nature of this event. I believe it has to do with our first conscious encounter with Death, that is, the dissolution of form. We saw suddenly that the bodies we had just discovered -and learned to love- were vulnerable to forces larger than us, and we became afraid.

sawdust. Similarly, the mind, when it is not resting in openness and awareness, will take all input and crush it into conformity with its rigid beliefs. It then amasses "evidence" and "data" confirming its worldview.

As sovereign creators, it is our inalienable birthright to experience the world according to our beliefs. Some of us prefer not to experience a world of darkness, suffering, and rigidity. We would like to create a life-narrative of inner peace and light. This is immanently possible. However, in the dominant culture of our Western world, our primary tool for "problem solving" is the mind. As noted above, if we try to use the mind to untangle the mess of stories, justifications, and thoughtforms that have been created over the top of our original moment of suffering, we become hopelessly lost in a dark, dense, and impenetrable maze. This is the temptation put forth by the powerful mechanism of the ego. It compels us into the maze of our beliefs, prodding us to defend, justify, convince, and prove the existence of God. The longer we spend caught in that web, the more lost, fearful, and frustrated we become.

Luckily, untangling the story isn't necessary. Refuting, debating, proving, justifying, and amassing evidence in order to claim the existence of the inner Eden is not necessary. It is not incumbent on us to convince anyone, including ourselves, that we are already worthy and whole. We can let go of the idea that receiving the peace of our being requires any effort whatsoever.

To know peace, to receive the promise of the New Eden, we must turn away from the mind and engage the heart as our guide. When we do this we lift, finally, the heavy mantle of self-blame that has been causing us untold, unnecessary misery throughout our entire lives. Our heart will offer the piercing light of hope that dissolves the maze completely. It invites us to give up the stories that trap us in misery and cycles of self-recrimination. Through the eye of the heart see ourselves in a new light- as one who has gained wisdom through suffering and is now ready to let the past rest. We claim our right not to let the past have power over us anymore. We declare that we will no longer be kept from our birthright of peace and harmony with all that is.

This declaration acts like a drop of water in a still pool. It naturally and effortlessly expands across the entire surface of the water. When we let our mind rest and finally accept the truth of our being, we can extend our heart's grace to all of the humans who have ever lived. We stop blaming ourselves and others for the trajectory of humankind. From the space of our heart- that pure place that lives beneath language, beneath words, and beneath reason- we can see with compassion and sincere remorse the imprint of unworthiness that humans have passed down like a heavy debt through the generations. We see the arc of our history anew. From this place of love, we can Reverse back to the beginning of time, take the shame-filled story of Adam and Eve - so deeply imprinted on the subconscious of our entire culture - and rewrite it as a story of innocence.

Clearly, re-writing the story of humanity's original "sin" requires a massive movement of the heart. The mind is not capable of forgiveness. The mind sees the world in terms of duality- right and wrong, good and evil. The mind is not, and never will be, our mechanism of our salvation. Alone, cut off from the vast spirit of the heart, the mind is a woefully inadequate, limited to repeating only what it knows, stuck in creating and recreating loops of suffering.

In order to re-write the story of humanity as one of love, courage, and redemption, we must turn away from our mind as the guiding force of our lives and embrace the fathomless love of the heart. The heart does not exist in a state of duality. It is an instrument only of oneness, of pure and effortless divine love. It alone can guide us beneath the layers of self-righteousness into the open horizon of freedom, compassion, and instantaneous redemption.

Forgiving the past may seem like an intimidating endeavor to undertake, but the process of re-writing the story of humanity offers itself as a natural and loving progression. We begin with the first, and perhaps hardest steps. We begin by forgiving ourselves- that wounded child who so long ago turned away from the light of love. We progress to forgiving those around us. We let go of the energy, the cords, the burdens we have taken on that are not and never have been ours. We use the wisdom of the heart to forgive and let go of those who have come in and out of our lives, those who have wronged and betrayed us. We see that their betrayal never truly had the power to hurt us.

As we continue to forgive, we understand that the heart lives already and always in effortless unity with all that is. We do not need to create this harmony; it already exists. All that is asked of us is to feel it. As we do so we progress, one by one, human by human, love by love, until all the world is redeemed.

This, at last, is one of the most joyful meanings of redemption: to harvest the fruit of your suffering by bringing that suffering into its ultimate, divine expression. When brought into the light of compassion, the many instances of suffering you experienced that stemmed from that one, first devastating trauma, suddenly blossom into wisdom- a fruit that can nourish the world. When we Reverse back to that first moment of pain, we do not change the past. Instead, we allow the past to rest simply as it is while we change fundamentally our relationship to all that has been. As we Reverse the story of humanity, we see that the pain and suffering and trauma never severed our connection with the light of the Divine. Instead, these experiences of suffering gave rise to inventions of pure grace.

Inventions Made in Darkness

It is important to understand that, in the long journey through darkness humans never truly forgot their divine origin. In our resilience, courage, devotion, and infinite creativity, we began, right underneath the nose of our egos, to build the tools we would need to merge back into a state of oneness. From within the deeply uncomfortable state of perceived separateness from God, humans invented three tools that have helped us, step by step, to reclaim our innate divinity. These tools were the "fruit" of Eve's disobedience, and we are currently in the process of mastering them as a collective.[5] They are:

Compassion
Discernment, and
Forgiveness

The difference between pre-apple humanity and humans after the Great Change (that is, the collective evolutionary leap from "survival" to "thriving") will be our enhanced state of conscious and self-referential awareness. It's important to note that pre-apple Adam and Eve *did* live in oneness and harmony with all things, but it was a state of purely unconscious oneness, much like the animal kingdom or an infant. Animals (and infants) live in perfect, amoral symbiosis with the Earth, but they do so without the capacity for self-reference. As such, they cannot consciously command their divinity to create.

If we imagine that pre-apple Adam and Eve existed in a state of oneness akin to the animal kingdom, then the qualities of compassion, forgiveness, and conscious discernment were not possible, nor were they necessary. All three qualities imply a necessary

---

[5] We have, in our infinite creativity, designed a universal curriculum for ascension from separation into oneness. I suspect that these "tools," which humanity has invented and mastered, will be our ultimate offering as a species to the expanded realms of existence. As humans draw back the veils and take their place as citizens within the wider galactic community, we will be able to offer to other species our own "pedagogy of the divine," that is, the inventions of forgiveness, compassion, and discernment that can be ordered and re-ordered in infinite ways to create a bridge from separation into oneness.

level of (perceived) separateness, just as all three, simultaneously involve an instantaneous bridging of that separateness.

Compassion

For instance, with compassion[6] one is able to know another deeply and hold their suffering without resistance, denial, intellectualization, or the impulse to "fix" anything. Compassion is a reaching out from the heart of the self to connect with another to hold them in strength, presence, understanding, and love. It is an acceptance of separation even as it discovers the natural, underlying thread of unity between two beings.

Discernment

Secondly, discernment, though it may seem like a quality that increases separation, is actually a necessary tool for defining the boundaries that allow for true intimacy. Discernment is the tool that helps us separate divine frequencies from egoic ones.

Before the introduction of the ego, all beings were guided entirely by unconscious instinct- a state which made discernment both unnecessary and impossible. With post-apple humanity came the ability to create anything at all. However, it remains a truth that any creation cannot help but reflect and perpetuate the state of consciousness of its creator. Therefore, humans who exist in a state of (perceived) separation cannot help but bring forth creations that

---

[6] I would like to note that "compassion" is not to be confused with "pity." Pity implies a subtle hierarchy where one is "better off" and the other "worse off." In this way, pity undermines sovereignty because it diminishes the other, thus reinforcing separation. Compassion, in contrast, is a gesture of the heart that reinforces connection. It holds the suffering as "our" suffering, in pure and loving understanding. In this way, we can agree with Yeats, in his poem "The Second Coming," that the divine is, in actuality, pitiless- though it is simultaneously merciful and full of compassion.

reflect and perpetuate separation. For the first time, then, poisons, toxins, parasites, and other life-draining creations burst into the world. In response, humans invented discernment in order to choose that which was life-giving and eschew that which was not.

Discernment is not to be confused with judgment. Judgment springs from an arbitrary assignment of morality, which perpetuates the false duality of "right" and "wrong." Instead, discernment is the exercise of free will in service to worthiness and self-love. Discernment is the ability to choose, without judgment, that which carries a life-force of its own and move away from that which, by unconscious but inevitable design, draws life-force away.

As we raise our consciousness and release from our being the entities and frequency patterns that carry no inherent life force (and thus drain *us* of *our* life force in order to survive), we will become very sensitive to the creations that were made "in sin."[7] With conscious discernment we will naturally be drawn to that which has been made in worship and, as such, carries a tangible light, energy, and life force of its own. We will be compelled to interact only with that which will amplify our own life-force. In this way, the more we allow ourselves to follow the path of non-judgmental but conscious discernment, the more quickly we draw ourselves toward higher and higher states of purity, clarity, vitality, and awareness.

Forgiveness

Lastly, forgiveness, the final and arguably most powerful tool of our salvation, implies a state of separation even as it acts at once to dissolve that separation. From an angelic state of awareness,

---

[7] As I will discuss in the section on Original Sin, *sin* simply means "without." I use it to refer to any creation that emerges from a state of separateness or, *without* the life force of the divine. These creations act as multi-dimensional parasites, as they contain no life force of their own and must therefore draw life from a host in order to exist.

forgiveness is incomprehensible, as no one could ever commit an act that could make the slightest impression on their pure offering of love. From a "fallen" state, however, forgiveness is the bridge back to unity with our divine nature. Forgiveness means that we release the cords of attachment that tie us to others. We allow the past to be in the past. We acknowledge all that has been, without blame or judgment, and resolve to move forward without carrying the dead weight of regret, doubt, or resentment.

The Lord's prayer offers in exquisite simplicity a template for realizing divine perfection. It is, in essence, a meditation on forgiveness- an articulated pathway to grace. When we read closely the familiar words, we see that the only thing that humans need to actually *do* to bring heaven to Earth is to unconditionally forgive our trespassers. If we can do that, the divine takes care of the rest.

Forgiveness is truly an invention of pure love- one that could only have been created in the depths of darkness from an indomitable will to return to the truth of our souls. True forgiveness is, in many ways, humanity's most potent tool for ascending beyond suffering.

But what *is* forgiveness? It is a mechanism, a gesture of the heart that is widely misunderstood. Like all actions that originate in the heart, true forgiveness cannot be grasped by the rational mind. Forgiveness is often viewed through the lens of the ego as something that we do "for" others. We have seen many examples of people magnanimously and publicly "forgiving" those who have wronged them. However, true forgiveness is not a public phenomenon, nor is it gratifying to the ego.

True forgiveness is, in fact, a dire threat to the ego. It obliterates our sense of righteousness, dissolves indignation, transcends "right" and "wrong," and places us firmly in a state of tranquil and empowered sovereignty. Forgiveness is a private, inward turning, a quiet acknowledgement of peace and space. It is declared through the subtle shift of the being away from blame and judgment. Forgiveness is a declaration of freedom born from self-love. It is not something we do for another, nor does it incur its own debts. Instead, it is the clear-eyed embracing of all that has been and a willingness to cultivate, with intention, the exact qualities you want to have and hold in the sanctuary of your own sacred heart.

Forgiveness does not mean you condone the behavior of another. It doesn't mean you have to welcome them into your life with open arms, strike up a friendship, or invite them to dinner. Instead, forgiveness is an exhale of relief. It is the effortless surrender of heaviness that must happen through holding the self in infinite tenderness. It is a cleansing waterfall of grace that descends through our lives, a force of nature that nothing can cling to. It ruthlessly washes away all that is dense, intractable, weary, and tense. It moves through us without apology, explanation, or justification. This waterfall flows at all times and can be invoked and entered into at any given moment.

Forgiveness is an opening of the hands, a release of the tightness and anger of "look what you did to me." It is an acknowledgement that the choices others have made have no bearing on our worth. It is a declaration that all lives are sacrosanct. True forgiveness severs any lingering energy of resentment, any energetic cords to those who have perpetrated against us. We do not need to even inform others that they have been forgiven, as this can often be an invitation to re-establishing a toxic connection. Instead, we let others choose their path and resolve not to interfere. We let go of needing to fix, change, or even explain the situation so that they can understand our point of view. We simply let go, let it be, and face both inward and forward, toward the light of our true self.

If people or situations resurface in our lives, we treat them with open-hearted kindness (and forgive *ourselves* when we stumble). We hold nothing against them, yet we do not owe them anything. We acknowledge as well that they owe nothing to us. They do not need to change to suit our preferences, and we do not owe them a place in our lives. In this way, through the active exercise of forgiveness, discernment, and compassion, we let the dignity and light of our hearts guide us toward that which is good and pure. And we gratefully let go of the rest.

Forgiving Eve

It is time to Reverse back in time and tap into the first moment at which humanity experienced separation from God, that is, the prophetic juncture at which Eve plucked the forbidden apple and took that first, legendary bite. Going back in time to unlock the original story of separation will crack open the portal to our ultimate salvation as a species.

Let's start by looking anew at Eve's motivation to eat the apple. In our own processes of personal Reversing, we can see the ways in which our actions are motivated by forces far larger and more complex than we can understand. The same was true for mythical Eve, who made the unilateral decision to plunge humanity through the veil of separation. We can understand now that she was the first to take up the mantle of free will by responding to the invisible, inevitable, and overpowering needs of human evolution.

There was, in short, a deep and driving hunger that she sought to satisfy with this mythical fruit. This hunger took the form of one irresistible question- the question that became Eve's legacy. It was the simple question, "I wonder…?"

Wonder is a phenomenon that appears with the expansion of consciousness. It is the ultimate question of the imagination- the ability to sense something beyond what is known. Wonder is what drives the attainment of all wisdom. The moment we muse, "I wonder?" we are confronted with the deepest question of evolution. Eve's "I wonder" was one of the biggest inquiries of all- the desire that launched us up and out of a state of unconscious oneness with the Earth and into a new phase of self-referential development. It was, in short: "I wonder what it is like to *know* I am God?"

Humans have been sinking their teeth into that question ever since. We can thank Eve now for daring to ask it. The desire to know we are God is *the* question that drives us ever onwards towards the pinnacle of existence. It is the relentless force behind our inevitable apotheosis. And we absolutely cannot - it is impossible- to stop until we reach it.

Of course, to *know* we are God we must first know a reality that seems devoid of Him. Claiming our divinity must be a choice or it is nothing at all. So, our prayers were answered. We were given the gift of choice.

From the moment Eve brought the apple to her lips, humanity seemed plunged into a dark and discordant reality full of suffering and pain and separation.[8] This period of darkness for humanity has been a long, long journey in accepting and wielding with wisdom the gift of our free will. Like a child being given a very dense, very difficult puzzle, we were handed all of the necessary pieces and have, ever since, been fitting them together.

The first piece we were given was our ego. Though often villainized, the ego is in actuality a precious gift, an unparalleled birthright without which the realization of our divine nature would be impossible. The ego is the part of us that is self-referential. It is what allows us to know ourselves. It is the mechanism that provides the opportunity for choice.

---

[8] This, I may note, is often the case when we embark on a new journey. Halfway in, when it is far too late to turn back, we raise our hands to the heavens and cry, "what was I *thinking* to get myself into this?!" There is, however, only one way to go. And when we think back to what drove us, the wisest of us accept that it could never have been otherwise.

For Adam and Eve, the archetypal mother and father of humanity, the gift of the ego - this sudden mirror of their own existence- was bewildering and frightening. Along with the ego came a sliver of separation, which was the witness looking upon the self. This allowed, for the first time, the capacity to judge, criticize, and blame. They looked at themselves and, having not yet developed eyes of compassion, were ashamed.[9]

It was the symbolic eating of the apple that brought free will into this very dense, very physical dimension. In some ways, the decision to eat the apple *was* the first free-will act. In this deeply symbolic story, there was perhaps nothing special about the fruit itself. It was the decision to defy "God" that helped humans finally understand our capacity to choose our reality. Disobedience (as any teenager will tell you), is a very clear and direct route to declaring independence. If all we ever do is follow the rules, how are we to know the difference between choice and compliance? How are we to know the difference between free-will and slavery?

So, Eve, wondering, disobeyed. And with that act she understood she was free. The ego was granted through this act of disobedience. As we defied "God," we were suddenly aware of our ability to choose our actions and reactions in the world. And, of course, with choice comes freedom.

True freedom is a vast and terrifying thing. With it, there is no one to turn to and no standard by which to measure rightness and wrongness. It is completely amoral and requires a corresponding vastness of self in order to be embraced and embodied responsibly. It is no wonder then, that upon discovering the extent of their own innate power, Eve and Adam's first reaction was to cover themselves

---

[9] This shame was not in any way alleviated by the false God-figure who cast them from Eden with curses and cruel threats. In some ways, I believe the false God figure must have been their own internal voices, that voice of fear and doubt that undermines joy- that voice that so many of us still heed as if it was God.

with fig leaves and cower in the shrubberies. It is very scary to discover that you inherently hold the power of God. Facing up to our inexorable freedom is the ultimate existential crisis, and it is this threshold that humanity is approaching *en masse*.

It has been put off for so long because this moment of dawning- this threshold of empowerment where we claim the birthright of our free and divine sovereignty- is the ego's worst nightmare.

The ego was given as a method for learning. Suffering (which is only experienced through the ego), results from repressing and hiding our vast, limitless, inherent freedom. Repression doesn't make the freedom go away, it just squishes our life force into the dense, trapped frequencies that manifest as fear and physical ailments. However, the ego, which consists of hidden and trapped reservoirs of life force, was designed from the beginning to self-destruct and, with the tremendous catalytic energy released from that dissolution, launch us into the next stage of awareness. The ego itself knows it, and has been for eons, attempting to put off that final moment of its own annihilation. The irony is, of course, that the more vehemently the ego resists, the more energy it builds for this final detonation, and the more it hastens its demise.

So, we stand at now at the threshold of resolution that was seeded in that first courageous bite. Humanity is poised on the brink of another evolutionary leap. We are being prepared to harvest the fruits of Eve's courageous legacy and return once again to the Garden. We are a new species, however. We have growth through suffering; we have evolved from naivete into innocence. We have chosen to fight our way from suffering to oneness, from separation to divinity. We have chosen our garden against all odds, and, seamed with battle scars, we accept it now as our unalienable birthright. We have become a species with a glint in our eye- the light of ironic humor and irreverent lightness, fearless and forevermore unphased, untroubled, and unmoved by the wily machinations of ego. We are, in short, a formidable species. After this, it will be very, very difficult to ever mess with humans again. Such are the fruits of disobedience. Such is the legacy of Eve.

Inner Eden: The Manifest Light of the Soul

The preceding section allowed us to reframe our story of evolution through the eyes of forgiveness, love, wonder, and an understanding of the wider arc in which humans live and evolve. As we consider our origin story, we can see it now as a movement of courage and curiosity, a prayer made in wonder, and an inevitable step on our journey to becoming God. We can see the way in which we chose to step out of the unconscious naivete of being in order to grow, evolve, and return back to oneness with all of the command of a sovereign creator. We can see that we have learned, grown, and evolved through darkness, moving always toward light, and never losing touch with the core truth of our being.

We can see that humanity is ready now to take the next leap of evolution out of the mind and into the sacred realm of the heart. We are ready to move beyond a reality defined by duality- light and dark, right and wrong, joy and pain, scarcity and abundance. We can let go of suffering as the only driving force for growth. In this way, we shift the goal of evolution from surviving to thriving. We can embrace the understanding that we are, ever and always, only love.

In so doing, we manifest Eden.

I would like to take now the wide, sweeping arc of time that we have traveled and bring it all back to the here and now- to your own precious life and the Eden you are destined to create around and within you.

The pure Eden of your being manifests when you follow your heart's deepest longings, your own personal, "I wonder." This wonder exists beneath distraction, addiction, and fleeting desire. This wonder is the living pulse of your life- the very reason you took form. This wonder is the longing draws you ever onwards toward the template of perfect peace that lives within you as both promise and destiny. These longings are the nameless questions that will not let you rest until you have lived them to the fullest.

Your questions are as relentless and unyielding as love. They will bring you again and again to the edge of your limits, leading you through fear, away from illusion, and into the truth of your self.

We see now that the mind cannot be our guiding light toward this inner Eden. Though a powerful mechanism for focused creation, the true nature of the mind can only be discovered when it lays itself down in service to the heart. The sphere of the heart is the ultimate instrument of manifestation, the divine voice that brings us out of prison and into the vast expanse of our freedom. When we follow our heart, we dissolve barriers of fear and illusion and discover our most effortless and joyful way of being. We find the ringing voice of our in-dwelling truth.

We see that the heart exists already and always in oneness. Your personal heart is a fractal of the universal sacred heart and therefore holds within it all of the secrets of the universe. When you quiet your mind and tap into our heart, you gain access to this limitless wisdom of Earth and wider cosmos. When you act from the heart, the sublime moves through you in one, unbroken ribbon of energy. You become stillness-in-action, moving in perfect unity with all that is.

As the heart leads us beyond fear, we finally tune into our natural rhythms of sleep and hunger, of labor and rest. Our rhythms (which are much slower and simpler than the current, frantic world would lead us to believe) move in perfect balance with the Earth and all of her creatures. When we allow this slow, steady, and unhurried internal rhythm to guide us, we come into harmony with our divine Mother. As more and more people allow the heartbeat of the Earth to synchronize with their own, the collective begins to evolve rapidly, coming into pace with each other and the natural resonance of the planet. This collective slowing down allows Eden to burst to life all over the world, naturally bringing the organic genius of each human into blossom.

The first garden we must tend, however, is the personal garden, the inner sanctuary of the self. The self is a fractal of all that is, so, when we tend to ourselves, we automatically tend to the Earth and one another. In this way, there is truly no higher calling than loving and tending to the self.

Humans are beginning to understand this now on a grand scale. We are ready, finally, to shed the burden of our past by re-telling the origin story of our humanity and the origin of our own innocent misunderstandings. We have mastered the tools of the heart- compassion, discernment, and forgiveness- and we are ready to use them to once and for all bridge the gap of separation that has for so long defined our existence. We are ready to view these past years of darkness, not as evidence of an inherent moral failing, but as a courageous journey back into the light. We are willing now to take ourselves- and all of humanity alongside us- up into our arms, to extend the gift of forgiveness, and finally allow all that has been to come to rest. We are ready to draw nutrients from the rich, dark soil of our suffering and grow into the light of divine awareness, manifesting our very highest expression in this body, in this lifetime.

We can see ourselves now as the ones who wondered, the ones who dared ask the question, "what would it be like to *know* I am God?" Our prayers were answered, and we answered them in turn with the full-bodied expression of our humanity. With eyes of forgiveness, we can see ourselves as children who walked undaunted through the dark and mazy passageways of fear, moving always back toward the light.

The butterfly's immediate path is erratic and unpredictable. If we tried to map its moment-to-moment movements, we would become frustrated and bewildered by the seeming inconsistency of it all. Yet butterflies migrate over wide swaths of distance. They are fragile, indestructible beings that strike out unhesitatingly over oceans and land at far-away destinations. Thus, the path of the butterfly is beautiful, erratic, and, when viewed from a higher and wider angle, perfectly constant.

In the same way, the trajectory of human evolution is like the path of the migrating butterfly. When we look at a small, concentrated piece of time, we seem erratic, unpredictable, and maddeningly chaotic. Yet, when we step back to take in the wider arc of our journey, we can see ourselves as fragile, indestructible beings who have been moving always toward that which is good and whole and true.

We have struck out over the ocean. We have found our way. All that has ever been is forgiven. We have arrived. It is time now to thrive.

Chapter 2: Awakening

In the following contemplations I offer personal stories and intimate understandings of life in the New Eden. These reflections were crystallized over the three years I spent attempting to make sense of the world after my first spiritual awakening. I offer nothing in this chapter that has not been tested and tested again through the laboratory of my own life.

After my own awakening, the voice of my heart gradually amplified within me. Over time, it felt as though I was seeing the world through new eyes- eyes that could see at the core of all the light of grace. Concepts or ideas that I had taken for granted would suddenly dissolve and reform in new ways. This process was so fascinating and so challenging that I gave myself up to it. I retreated within. My entire life became a living experiment in which I followed threads of doubt, pain, suffering, self-recrimination, shame, and that ever-present wonder back and back until I was satisfied that I had touched upon the origin of it all. From this place- this bedrock of existence- I was able to find new ways to make sense of the world, of my life, and the whirl of chaos that seems to hold all of this planet in sway.

As you read you will see again and again the one truth on which I found I could rely. This truth is the drumbeat beneath my words; it emerges as an unmistakable golden thread woven through all of the proffered reflections. It is the one premise, tested over and over again, from which all of my contemplations flow: namely, the divine is all-loving, unconditionally supportive, and ever-present. The divine *is* us. There is nothing we could ever do, or have ever done, that could remove, separate, or take us away from the divine. God is love; humans are God, ergo, humans are love. All else is illusion.

I make no apology for the shifting tone and cadence of these contemplations. My writing will often take on the frequency of the transmission itself, shifting like the weather, the sun, the river, the seasons. Some contemplations called for a more didactic expression, others a lilting, even poetic voice. All have been honed like diamonds by the pressures of time, experience, precision, and reflection.

If I did this right, these contemplations will open a window for you to peer at the world through my eyes, seeing it as I see it. You do not need to agree nor resist my perspective. You can simply allow or let go according to the guidance of your own higher self. Overall, I hope these contemplations serve you as you transition into your highest expression and discover your own divine gifts

Self and World

Those of us awakening to our inner divinity are finding it increasingly difficult to live and work within the systems that currently run our world. These systems no longer reflect our understanding of who we are. They no longer reflect or uphold the level of consciousness that we, as forerunners of the new era, have stepped into. The prevailing systems on our planet can no longer support the expansion that humanity is undergoing. They are like training wheels or an old textbook that we have already mastered. I speak of systems of government and justice, of education and economics, of industry and business. All of these are models that were formed at previous levels of evolutionary consciousness. They are rapidly becoming irrelevant and indeed untenable. They cannot take us where we are inevitably headed.

The structures founded on old assumptions and old levels of consciousness must (and inevitably will) be released and transformed. The unstoppable force of evolution guarantees this. However, we have a choice as to how we release them. If we don't release them with love and clear-eyed openness then these systems will self-destruct on their own, causing much more suffering than is necessary. I do not speak, therefore, of revolution or reformation, but of ascension.

Those of us who have experienced the Great Change within ourselves have already come (or are rapidly coming) to embody the new consciousness. We stand therefore at the threshold, at the hinge of this transition as the welcome committee. We are the ones who can create the practical structures, curricula, pathways, and bridges that bring people and systems into this new way of being without the need for fear, destruction, resistance, or suffering. We can do this because we have undergone the transition ourselves on a personal level. As such, we understand the process intimately. With our embodied wisdom, we have already begun breaking trail, creating a bridge to for others to follow into the realm of the heart. We understand, because we experienced it, that the mind is not the mechanism through which these new systems will develop, as the mind, with its assumption of duality, is the very instrument that we are transcending.

The majority of organizations and the network of our global systems were formed at a previous level of evolution upon a set of assumptions that are no longer relevant or true. The systems currently in place emerged from humanity's need for survival. They were founded on assumptions of scarcity, lack, mistrust, and the desire for protection from violent, brutal, and self-serving *others*.

These systems emerged from the belief that love itself is a finite and precious resource and must therefore be controlled, suppressed, and defined within narrow constructs, directed only toward a worthy few. In this old way of being, there is self and there is other. Those whom we love stand in contrast to those whom we fear and distrust. We have felt the need to protect the self, family, and close loved ones at the expense of others. As a result, humanity has been enacting a long-term tragedy of the commons, fearfully grabbing at resources, constructing barriers to ward off "the other," and building up defenses against famine and death. This drama of love and fear, control and denial has been played out for many generations. The need to protect ourselves has been overlaid onto our being, expressing through our psyche, our body, and our very DNA so that it would seem to be the truth of our nature. But I tell you, it is not who we are.

As we awaken, we become aligned with divine will, which moves according to the limitless sphere of the heart. This heart-sphere is the connecting fascia of all beings on Earth. When we align our frequency to the heart, we see that, while each person and each being may express as an individual, each being on Earth is inextricably and unbreakably connected. This connection is true whether we believe in it or not. To deny our inherent connection would be similar to saying that a finger or hand is not part of the body. Each human, while individual, is also part of the larger body of the Earth.

The connected heart-sphere, where a part of us always resides, recognizes that any suffering on the planet belongs to- and is experienced by- the whole. Humans exist as one organism- one sheath of consciousness on the planet. In this understanding we can accept all other humans as self. Every impulse, every emotion, every action undertaken by another is an impulse, action, or emotion of self. Those whom we cannot forgive or to whom we close our hearts simply represent an aspect of self we cannot love. In this way, the forerunners carrying the frequency of the New Eden will express their courage through openness, fearlessness, honesty, transparency, and vulnerability to in order to break down barriers of protection and love all as the self.

The gravitational pull of the status quo, the relentless "isness" of suffering, and the hungry-hungry hippo-reality we have created holds immense influence over our psyche. Yet, it is ultimately fragile. Our role as leaders is not to deny, resist, or escape the status quo nor the systems that exist, but to engage with them from a quiet place of knowing. The divine spark within us, the divinity that *is* us, has no need to compromise, bargain, appease, or convince. Without resistance, without judgment, and without effort, the light of our being illuminates what is unacceptable, and our natural light provides a way for the will, resources, and miracles to materialize in the physical realm to restore that which is out of balance.

As we awaken to our innate divinity and unlimited capacity to command miracles, we will no longer relate to a world run by assumptions of fear and lack. We no longer consider "survival" as the ultimate goal of life. In the coming Eden, we will break away from evolutionary models designed purely for survival and create instead models designed for thriving. We ask a new question: "what would the world look like if it was ordered for thriving?" We begin to understand that true thriving is a collective phenomenon and not something that can be realized only by a few.

When we see that thriving can only occur collectively, as a planetary phenomenon, we begin to view the entire world as our responsibility. We see all humans, and all beings, as having an unconditional right to live lives of meaning, freedom, abundance, fulfillment, and love. We become prepared, not to force the world to bend toward our personal notions of justice and righteousness, but to shift ourselves to become a living embodiment of thriving. As we do so, we naturally prepare the collective and our global systems to evolve to match this new way of being- a way of being rooted in unconditional love, abundance, connectedness, and worthiness.

In this, we show a way beyond conflict, a path that transcends "us versus them." We know that, in all things, there is always a way forward that will offer benefit to all- such is the superpower of the heart. In this faith we become a cadre of creative, inspired wayshowers who seek and seek and seek until that wholesome, heart-inspired solution is discovered. We will know it because it resonates with a rightness, a wholeness, a truth that cannot bend to fear.

In this, we assume command even as we relinquish control. We understand "command" as a responsive, self-possessed way of moving in the world, and we let go of control, which is a weak stance, full of resistance, fear, rigidity, and blindness. We see that true leaders do not need to control anything. Instead, they assume command in resonance with divine will and the highest mind.

In aligning with the divine nature of our humanity, we reframe the world as a place of abundance, freedom, transparency, and generosity, where all beings are unconditionally worthy and are wholly supported to manifest their highest potential. In a world that has for so long delineated "haves" from "have-nots," in a world terrified that there will never be enough (translated "enough for *me*"), this way of being demonstrates radical growth in consciousness and the ultimate leap from fear into faith.

As we align with the intelligence of the heart, we understand that with all questions there is always a higher perspective. There is always a solution available that will serve the highest good of all. This perspective resolves conflict, not through compromise or reason, but through transcending the duality that led to conflict in the first place.

We understand, and accept, that the transcendent solution will always come at the cost of certain of our attachments. As we seek these solutions, as we transcend duality, we lean into the very truth of our being. Those of us who place love above fear will seek these solutions even as they dissolve our identification with the small, fearful things to which we have clung for so long. We recognize that these small things, these attachments, can no longer guide us into our inevitable expansion. We trust that when we give truly, we give always and only to ourselves, and when we receive, we open to a flow of joy, worthiness, and generosity.

I was once gifted with a vision of our Earth. In my vision, the Earth became a sinuous being, glowing star-bright and red in the cosmos. The divine joined it, an identical sinuous being radiating ineffable white light. Together they danced, the Earth and the divine, like tango dancers. I saw them as Earth and God; human and divine; ego and the light of Source, cleaving so closely that not a sliver of space lay between. Every time ego took an erratic or unexpected step, the divine was there, stepping in perfect and graceful alignment. I watched as every movement of ego was transformed into ecstatic dance.

That image burst on me like a revelation. I finally understood that no choice we make has the power to take us away from the divine. There is not one aspect of our planet or our lives that is out of reach of grace. Higher love is always there, perfectly in step, never caught off balance, never flustered, separated by not a single breath of space.

The ramifications of this revelation are enormous. It means that nothing we've ever chosen has been a mistake. We have nothing to regret, and we can truly do no wrong. The understanding that there has never, for one moment, been a wrong choice in all of the history of the world came upon me like a cleansing waterfall of grace. All is, and has always been, forgiven.

There was more, however. It wasn't just the vision itself, but the way it came upon me. It was the music that created this vision, you see. A violin was playing, and I saw the music streaming from the meeting of bow and strings like light, and that light wrapped around our whole Earth, turning this thumping, wild, chaotic melee into a rapturous dance.

In that moment I understood something else. I understood that each of us holds our own resonance, our own very specific frequency. When we find it, when we refine it, when we sing it out, it resolves chaos to reveal the divine harmony that moves within ourselves and on Earth. This is our unmistakable songline, our gift to the chorus of humanity. When we merge with the pure resonance of self, we understand that we aren't here to change the world or each other; we're here to *dance*. And, as we can all attest, it is very hard to dance without music! So, it is our internal harmony, sent brightly and unselfconsciously into the world, that brings order to chaos, balance to wildness, and reveals the higher, transcendent symphony of all that is.

In the midst of a cacophony sometimes it takes just one, clear note to resolve the discordant noise into music. That one, clear, note: that is you. That is me. Our purpose is to bring ourselves into wholeness, so that each of us can shine that one, unequivocal signal out into the world.

And then, we dance.

Money

Money is like rain, like love, like breath. We do not hold our breath for fear of not receiving another inhale. We do not cling to the rain for fear that it will never fall again. Truly, no aspect of this world is beyond the reach of the divine hand; this includes our material needs and comforts.

As we come into alignment with our divine purpose, money becomes like a river flowing in the background. It is simply there for us when we need it. When we are thirsty, we dip our bucket and drink our fill. We do not concern ourselves with whether or not the river will dry up, and we do not waste time storing water.

The heart is universally free, existing beyond all constructs, all illusions, and all thoughtforms. It has the capacity to create from nothing. To what extent do we trust our hearts to provide for us? To what extent can we trust that our needs will be met when we break from the accepted mode of doing things?

Currently, assumptions governing money lead us to believe it must be "earned" through the betrayal of self, through giving our life, our presence, and our light to endeavors that are not fulfilling and, indeed, harmful. We believe money can only come in small, regular, and meted parcels as an established exchange of our time and skills. We turn away from our hearts with a shrug, saying, "I would be free, but I have to pay the bills." As though our heart, the very force that created us, is not capable of paying the bills! We have set ourselves up to choose between money and health, money and fulfillment, money and peace, as though these things cannot abide in the same place.

To break from these illusions, each of us must inevitably confront our deeply-embedded fear of lack. When we do this, as we turn toward money as a spiritual teacher, we will eventually walk the Earth as living proof that our needs can be met, and our lives provided for without self-betrayal. Indeed, in the coming era any poverty of soul will be reflected in our financial state. All is coming into alignment, and we will discover that turning away from our hearts will ultimately lead to the very debt we fear.

On the path to ultimate freedom, we can expect to come again and again to the decision point of self-betrayal. Each time we choose to uphold our deepest values of dignity, divinity, and self-worth, regardless of the circumstances, we set aside for ourselves unimaginable riches. As we embrace the path of our heart, we will see that we are worthy of the joy that it yields even as we find ourselves needing less and less. We will learn to accept the given fact of our prosperity with wonder, gratitude, and grace. We will give without fear and receive without guilt, until, ultimately the giving and receiving merge into one.

Embodiment

I wonder if you can take a moment now to behold your body. Your hands perhaps holding this book. The miracle of your muscles and tendons, the exquisite architecture of your ankles and feet. The manifest divinity of your face and throat. Even your aches and pains offer a message from beyond this realm. Our physical bodies are far more magical than we understand. Every cell of our bodies is intentional. We have been formed from a sacred geometric template and, as such, not one aspect of our bodies is an aberration or a mistake. Our bodies are the physical expression of our soul, and when we tune into our bodies to listen for its wisdom, we can find entirely new vistas of understanding about the nature of reality.

Currently, from our western medicinal systems to the dominant way of life in this culture, the body, when considered at all, is seen largely as an inconvenience. We spend much time, energy, and innovation devising ways to force the body to conform to accepted norms that deny the body's needs and, in many ways, its very existence. From school to the workplace, the body is considered primarily to be a vehicle for carrying the brain from one point to another. It is a means of productivity, and, when ill or out of balance, a nuisance that prevents us from doing more important and productive things. We spend much of our time denying, suppressing, or drugging into submission the body's natural rhythms, desires, and needs.

The Great Change that is upon us will not occur in spite of the body, but through it and because of it. The New Eden is the way of the body. It will offer a way of living that unconditionally loves, honors, listens to, and tends to the body as holy. In these coming times, we will finally recognize the body, not as a dense thing to be transcended, but as the most advanced form of spiritual technology in the universe.

We talk of "higher" planes as though they are something exclusive to this physical realm. Our bodies, however, are spirit made flesh. They are an unfathomable feat of divine will. They are spiritual creation moved into being by the power of our soul. Our bodies are perfect holograms of the higher dimensions, channeled into form through the physical laws of this realm. In short, our bodies are miracles, and they are capable of miraculous things.

The body is perfectly constructed to interact with this world of form while also maintaining communication with subtle, multi-dimensional aspects of existence. We live within a highly-attuned receiver, capable of picking up and manifesting the most exquisitely-refined frequencies of the Universe. People have demonstrated the capacity of the body to miraculously heal itself. We have seen examples of people living on nothing but prana, and there are people on Earth who have lived in the same body for hundreds of years. Far more than a plodding "meat suit," (as I have heard it horrifically described) the body is a rare and refined example of spiritual innovation that deserves to be honored, loved, cared for and yes, worshipped, with the highest levels of tenderness and devotion.

Many of us on Earth, and especially those of us reading this book, will have had a difficult time adjusting to the density of their bodies on this planet. It can be hard for us, who are accustomed to lighter plains of existence, to accept that we belong here. We often view our bodies and its needs and pain with distaste and frustration.[10]

---

[10] If I may be permitted a generalization, I believe this adjustment is particularly difficult for those who incarnated as men. Until such a time as duality is completely transcended, men offer an externalized, manifested form of the masculine energy, which is traditionally guided by reason, linear thinking, and structure. Men, therefore, often have more trouble connecting with their bodies. They will more often view their bodies as a means to an end as opposed to a sensory offering of pleasure or love. Women, in contrast, possess more access points, rhythms, and natural inclinations to inhabit the body with presence and pleasure.

One of the most simple and powerful decisions we can make on this spiritual journey is to finally admit that we are human. We were not mistakenly put here as a punishment or penance; this lifetime isn't simply a waypoint, and there isn't anywhere better to get to.

Accepting this truth allows us to claim our humanity as a high honor, opening the way to explore our humanity with curiosity and reverence. As we explore our humanity, we will come over and over again back to the mysteries of the body. The soul, after all, is formless. Therefore, it is the body that makes us human. In this way, we understand that the secrets of humanity must exist within the body itself. Our bodies are exquisite masterpieces wrought by a master hand, and they serve as testimony to the power of our soul's will. The body is the key to all knowledge, all evolution, and all of the secrets of this planet, and it is through our bodies that the New Eden will manifest.

Divine Union of Masculine and Feminine

I find it impossible to talk about embodiment without referring to the fundamental framework of manifestation, namely, that of the masculine and feminine energies.

As mentioned in relation to the garden, masculine energy refers broadly to order, structure, rationality, linearity, and precision. It is the aspect of self that simplifies, clarifies, and takes action. It is also the aspect of self that is associated with the mind. Masculine energy encompasses reason, thinking, and unmanifested spirit- in short, the part of us that is not the body itself. The feminine aspect of self is all that is manifested. The body, therefore, is the most feminine facet of our existence.

The dominant world culture, characterized by the wounded masculine, has prioritized, emphasized, and validated the masculine aspect of being (mind, reason, and thought) at the expense of the feminine side of our nature. Because the wounded masculine deploys its energy in dividing and conquering, it set up the other half of existence, the feminine, as a threat. Under this aegis the body, the most feminine aspect of our being, has been regarded with suspicion and wariness as a source of fear, unpredictability, and limitation. The body seems subject to laws beyond our control, and when the mind cannot control something, it becomes scared and reacts with judgment, suppression, and a frantic need to "figure it out." In the past 13,000 years of patriarchal rule, the body (and thus all of manifested form, including the Earth itself) has been denigrated, mistrusted, and generally viewed as either a burden,[11] or something to be conquered and controlled. In this way, the body has been set up as a barrier to the higher realms of heaven and light- the formless and therefore more desirable echelon of existence.

This view is subtly and pervasively reinforced by translations of ancient texts that form the very fabric of our consciousness. Buddhism has been interpreted as a process of clearing karma in order to exit the wheel of samsara, which binds us to the punishment of incarnating into form. The Bible itself, whether by design or carelessness, elevates, through emphasis and omission, the masculine principle (the spirit) over the feminine half of our being (the body and the Earth).

The unquestioned desirability of ascending beyond the body is even an underlying assumption of many non-religious, non-dogmatic, new-age spiritual movements, which elevate the "inner planes," star families, and "fifth dimensional reality" above what we

---

[11] See Yeats' poem, "Sailing to Byzantium," where he described his spirit as "fastened to a dying animal." Or in "The Tower," railing against the process of aging that "has been tied to me/ As to a dog's tail?" He captures well the masculine anguish of feeling the contours of the body as confining.

experience as "third dimensional reality." There is a subtle disparagement of the third dimension, which is distastefully referred to as "dense," as though our presence here is somehow "lower." Many people believe they are incarnating into this dimension to save the Earth from its own physicality.

We are not here to move beyond this dimension but to remove the veil from between the third dimension and all of the others. As we do this, our third-dimensional flesh can be realized as holy, and our third-dimensional experiences can be celebrated as gifts. The third dimension is, after all, completely unique in the vibrating spectrum of existence, and as such it has much to teach us. To concentrate the limitless universe into finite form is an absolute masterstroke of divine creativity, and it provides unparalleled opportunities for conscious expansion.

As feminine energy rises, heals, and comes into balance with the masculine, new texts in many wisdom traditions are coming to light that reiterate reverence for the body. One such example is the *Essene Gospel of Peace*.[12] This gospel features, immediately after the Lord's Prayer that is so familiar to us, another prayer in exactly the same format and cadence. However, this prayer is for the Earth, that is, the Mother. This prayer was placed in prominence next to the Lord's Prayer, in equal power and status. It is translated thus:

> Our Mother which art upon Earth, hallowed be thy name.
> Thy kingdom come, and thy will be done in us as it is in thee.
> As thou sendest every day thy angels, send them to us also.
> Forgive our sins as we atone for all of our sins against thee.
> And lead us not into sickness, but deliver us from all Evil.

---

[12] A series of texts unearthed from the Vatican library and translated by Edmond Bordeaux Szekely.

For thine is the Earth, the body, and the health. Amen.[13]

    The kingdom, the power and the glory, and the Earth, the body, and the health. With the pairing of the Lord's Prayer, and the prayer of the Earth Mother, we can begin to see humans as the divine children begotten of the union of Spirit and Earth. As their holy children, we hold within us the unfathomable power and love of each entity. Our limitless consciousness comes from Father Spirit, our bodies are of the Earth Mother, and our whole, complex being is the perfect union of these two divine entities. Within our formless spirit we hold the kingdom, the power, and the glory, and within our bodies we hold the miraculous consciousness and creative capacity of the Earth herself.

    When viewed through this lens, the human body, far from being a mistake or a burden, is, in fact, a perfect hologram of the Earth Mother. It is therefore an instrument of boundless and miraculous creativity. Our bodies were created from the consciousness of the Earth and therefore hold her vast and limitless intelligence. The same intelligence that designed the transformation of the butterfly and water cycle lives within us, at our fingertips (literally), to be discovered, harnessed, and explored.

    We begin to understand that a soul could not have incarnated into such an advanced form without exhibiting deep levels of mastery and knowing. As we understand that nothing is impossible, we can begin to wonder what our bodies are truly capable of in this coming era.

    It will be a revolution when our way of life becomes ordered around the needs and health of the body. In these coming times we will learn to treat the body, and all manifested forms, as holy, wondrous, and unmistakably intelligent.

---

[13] Szekely, Edmond Bordeaux (1977). *The essene gospel of peace: Book one.* Academy Books: San Diego, California.

This will not happen without choice, action, and courage. We stand in a system that has placed the masculine aspect- the intellect of the mind- as the ultimate force for understanding. Loving the body as sacred in a system that treats it largely as a problem will require practice, commitment, and courage. It will require aware and compassionate vigilance as we examine our lifestyle, habits, diets, and daily rituals. We must practice trusting the body as a wise and wholly intelligent instrument, capable of leading us into thriving. Again, our souls have alighted perhaps in countless manifestations throughout its life cycle. It is our bodies, made of Earth, that make us human. Therefore, the secrets of humanity live within the body itself. But to access these secrets we must trust, and we must choose.

In this way, feminine power and the rising of the sacred intelligence of the body is not an abstract concept but a real and manifested way of living. We must understand that the true rising of feminine power heralds a dramatic shift in all aspects of life as we allow our systems to bend in order to support the needs of manifested form- the body, the animals, and the Earth herself.

As a final note, though encouraging in many ways, we cannot point to growing numbers of women in power as irrefutable evidence of changing times. Many women who have risen to power in our extant systems have done so by adopting hyper-masculine personas. We will know that feminine energy is truly beginning to lead when we see new, creative, supportive, and *systemic* approaches to meeting the deep needs of the body and Earth.

Men and Women

We discussed masculine and feminine energies, but a contemplation on embodiment would not be complete without discussing the *embodied* manifestations of these energies on Earth, that is, men and women and the seemingly eternal conflict between them.

In the new era, the age-old battle of the sexes will eventually resolve into harmony. This will not happen, however, through compromise, repression, and just trying to "get along." I believe we must finally "have it out," in such a way that all of the pain, betrayal, and cruelty of the ages is finally expressed and yes, fully heard on both sides without reproach, condemnation, justification, or denial. Only then, when each of us feels fully seen and heard, will we stop escalating and subside finally into peace.

To find resolution it may be helpful to examine the underlying mechanisms that continue to perpetuate the battle of the sexes.

All manifested forms on Earth are reflections of the subtle and universal frequencies that our consciousness can access. As our consciousness darkened and constricted into a narrow band of frequencies, so too did our Earth become denuded of certain expressions of form. As humans expand in consciousness we will see new forms, species, and manifestations occurring on the planet that reflect our growing levels of access to wider and more refined bands of frequencies. Men and women, male and female, are embodied representations of the most fundamental energies of the universe: masculine and feminine; stillness and movement; order and chaos; death and life, respectively.

As we contemplate embodiment as an expression of divine worship, we must address this volatile subject of men, women, and particularly, of sexual relationships. This topic is central to a text that dares take on the question of our evolution of consciousness as a species.

The battle of the sexes has raged for eons as perhaps the fundamental conflict of humanity (starting of course with that primordial rift between Adam and Eve). In many ways, the conflict between men and women has been perpetuated by a refusal to accept the natural process by which life evolves.

As we transition into evolution for thriving, as opposed to evolution merely for survival, we will come to accept that the direction and catalytic energy of our evolution lies with women. This was another truth revealed by Eve- as a woman, it was her natural role to galvanize the process of movement from one state of being to another. Once again, as we transition into the era of Christ Consciousness, it will be the energy and power of the feminine, the fearless movement of change and adaptation, that leads the charge. It will also, as we shall see, be masculine acceptance of this fact that leads finally to harmony.

The accepted theory of evolution taught in the Western world focuses on "natural selection," that is, the "survival of the fittest." Animals who adapt to their surroundings throughout the generations will "survive," while more rigid species will die away. This comfortable theory not only focuses on survival as the ultimate goal of evolution, but it glibly passes over the other powerful force that guides our evolution, that is, sexual selection.

As women grow empowered in the world – materially, financially, emotionally, psychologically, and spiritually- "survival of the fittest" stands poised to be overshadowed by the process of sexual selection, which is the primary mechanism by which humans will evolve for thriving.

Needless to say, the rise to prominence of sexual selection as the primary force of evolution is a terrifying prospect for the unawakened man, as the process of evolution must finally be admitted to be out of his hands entirely. At this shift the role he had been playing becomes obsolete as the services he traditionally (ostensibly) offered (protection, material security, provisions, physical safety, etc.) cease to be needed. The unawakened man therefore feels a vague and nameless terror at the rise of feminine power. The more he is identified with his "traditional" role, the more threatened he will be by the changes, and the more he will kick, scream, fight, and gnash his teeth at the prospect of it.

While we can talk reasonably about the fact that men and women both carry the energy of the masculine and feminine (which is true), it remains a fact that women are the ones who conceive and bear life. Masculine and feminine energies take form on Earth as men and women, despite the fact that we each carry both frequencies within us. In the past two centuries, women worldwide have come rapidly through a testing ground in which they broke out of their rigidly-defined roles and explored the heretofore forbidden opposite frequency. Women, *en masse,* have enjoyed developing their masculine aspect and men, likewise, have enjoyed a relaxation of their own rigid, traditional role to become more comfortable with their feminine energy.

The men and women who have explored and mastered these polarities are moving now into a space where they can move fluidly within and between both aspects and rest, finally, in whichever role feels most natural. While virtuosos of both realms, as manifested aspects of masculine and feminine, the majority of men will feel most at home in their masculine energy, and the majority of women will feel most at home resting in their feminine energy. The model of a harmonious relationship between the sexes (defined first by a harmonious relationship within the self) requires simultaneous acceptance and transcendence of this most fundamental expression of duality. And this model of harmony, after centuries of bitter conflict, is finally beginning to emerge on the planet.

At this time, women can begin to accept, without contempt, fear, apology, or denial the natural biological power that they hold as bearers of life and the arbiters of who does, and does not, pass on their genes. As women do this, they dramatically shift the rules of a game that has been played fiercely and desperately up until now.

We can see how the patriarchy formed as an attempt to subvert women's natural power and responsibility as determiners of evolution. We can see the ways in which, over the centuries, women's sexuality became a closely-guarded commodity, with marriages and lineages decided upon by men. Instead of women freely choosing the qualities that would flourish in the species, we saw this natural law co-opted through tight and constrictive social norms and justified through systemic structures of shame and oppression. It is important to note here that, within structures of oppression, all beings suffer. The patriarchy built its own prison walls in which everyone, men and women, rich and poor, were encased.

Whether we like to admit it, even now in these progressive times mates are often chosen (at least in part) for their ability to provide material security, which has been elevated as a desirable trait in a partner. In a world that still trumpets the existence of scarcity and lack, and in a culture where the nuclear family is still the primary unit for procreation and the raising of children, selecting a mate who can buffer the hardships of poverty remains an appealing criterion.

In the new era of consciousness, however, humans will come to understand that abundance and prosperity are not the rational and linear functions of a system but immediately accessible to all people at any time. Through the ineffable quantum field, with which our heart is perfectly aligned, the means to provide for oneself will become as easy, effortless, and joyful as reaching up and plucking fruit from a tree. As we come into resonance with our divinity, we will finally understand the limitless power of our heart to provide, both spiritually and materially, for all of our needs without condition, effort, compromise, or the need for it to be "earned." As this happens, our way of life will shift dramatically into a state of unfettered freedom.

In throwing off the shackles imposed by systems of lack, in trusting that our heart's journey will bring us all of the prosperity we need in the right way and at the right time, we are able to relinquish fear, worry, and strategy about how to support ourselves. We can follow the voice of the heart without compromise. We can make decisions, not according to what is "reasonable" or "safe," but according to our deepest values. As women freely choose mates (or not) depending on values such as self-worth, dignity, and unconditional love, the course of human evolution will shift and accelerate dramatically.

As humans face up to and transcend their fear of scarcity, we will see dramatic shifts in the ways that we live together. We will recognize the nuclear family as an economic unit as opposed to a unit that is truly supportive of life. We will begin to naturally form into fractals, that is, supportive and synarchistic groups (or villages) that share and support each other in their unique, and aligned, purposes. These "villages" will not be tribal, as they were in the past, but drawn together by an unmistakable frequency pattern of symbiosis, living in harmony, as opposed to conflict and competition, with other groups.

As humanity moves into a state of effortless freedom and prosperity, we will not give up our natural form. That is, we will still, for the foreseeable future, incarnate as men and women holding the various powers and inclinations of our sex. We will, however, experience profound and irrevocable shifts in the ways that we relate to one another. This will be most visible in our experience of sexual desire.

As we move into the sanctuary of our heart, sexual desire will transform. It will be lifted from the realm of fear and brought through the heartspace, flowing powerfully as a wellspring of culminated life force, an endless river of inspiration and energy. We will be liberated from sexual desire as a driving and frantic need and will instead learn to embrace it as a dance of devotion and worship. Sex itself will become prayer, an ecstatic act of divine love that originates from the heart. We will become present to the life force within us and learn to command it, not through repression and denial, but through acceptance, joy, and presence. This transcendence of sexual desire will happen naturally as we continue to release anything and everything that prevents us from merging with our own ultimate state of oneness.

I would like to end this contemplation on embodiment with a reflection on masculinity. With all of the emphasis on feminine power, it is crucial that we examine the process by which the masculine (represented in form by incarnated men) is healing deeply and coming into humble resonance with the vast, unfathomable forces of the higher mind.

As we turn toward the feminine as a guiding power in the New Earth, masculinity, and men in general, have become villainized. We point vaguely toward "patriarchy" as the perpetrator of untold brutality, and, as there is no method of gaining a pound of flesh from a theoretical construct, we turn toward men themselves to pay the debt with their own skin.

Anger, rage, and deep, deep grief are natural in these times when all is surfacing to be seen, accepted, forgiven, and healed. However, blame, shame, and resentment only serve to reinforce the very cycles that have perpetrated cruelty. The times of suffering and darkness that humans have come through, the shadow frequencies that have engulfed our planet for so long, are the fault of no one. Humanity is a whole entity, an attuned instrument, a reflection of one unified consciousness of the Earth. If there was (is) conflict, strife, brutality, and cruelty it was (is) a product of the impersonal frequencies that have lain heavy on our world and within our psyches. We are clearing these now, together. Once all is brought forward, we must then let it all go.

In many ways, the whole human race is emerging from a long period of self-inflicted abuse. As we do this, men especially, as the incarnated beings that held some of our most violent frequencies, and, as such, perpetuated atrocities such as war, rape, genocide, and oppression, are beginning to truly feel the effects of this long, long cycle of brutality.

Men have been no less wounded by the patriarchy, yet, as perpetrators of the system, they do not know where to turn for relief. The ones awakening often feel that the darkness of the world must somehow be their fault, and this plunges them into a state of deep and reactive guilt. They do not have the ostensible moral high ground of victimhood to retreat to. We see a number of responses to this awakening. I highlight here three of the primary responses that I have experienced personally in men.

The first camp is a denial of the effects of centuries of systemic brutality and a refusal to feel the depth of suffering that was a result of these systems. With this response we see people, and men especially, become intractable in their positions, retreating into defensiveness and enacting desperate grabs for some guise of victimhood. We see fusillades flung from one trench to another as people build and defend whole identities around being wronged. This is the most fearful response and is perpetuated by people living in abject terror of the overwhelming nature of grief and the deep, bottomless pit of despair that exists in that dark, lonely place of separation.

As women take up the responsibility and power of directing evolution, the men in this fearful camp will inevitably react. We must be ready for the ensuing backlash that will try any means to undermine the developing power and will of the rising feminine. This group will use manipulation, attack, insults, gaslighting, self-righteousness, and the moral high ground to make us question ourselves and our decisions. We may see physical violence, but more likely it will take the insidious and manipulative tactic of using immanently reasonable-sounding justifications to point out all of the ways in which women are wrong to stand in their truth and power.

The traditional role of women in marriage, relationships, and communities has been to manage the emotions of all involved. If a relationship wasn't harmonious, it has traditionally been the woman's role to compromise, bend, and do all in her power to make sure everyone is soothed and happy, usually at cost to her own wellbeing. Over time, women have internalized this role to the point where many feel reactively guilty, at fault, and responsible if the people to whom they're close are emotionally distraught.

This will be the most potent weapon of the disenfranchised man- he will be very, very unhappy and he will blame her- either overtly or through subtle insinuations. This tactic is as unconscious as it is effective as, through the centuries, an unhappy man could mean punishment and even death to a woman in his thrall. As women take up their place in the changing world, they will be asked to face and overcome this deeply- embedded fear. She may be called arrogant and selfish. She may be called all sorts of things. We will see desperate attacks on women's rights, especially related to marriage and procreation. We must be ready to see this as a sign of progress and to calmly remain standing in our truth.

Remember that the divine never speaks through judgment. Your heart will never condemn you. When you hear these things, and see these things, know it is not your heart speaking, but the wounded ego of man. You are under no obligation to listen. We do not need the permission or approbation of any other human being in order to thrive.

So, we will be asked to stand our ground in the face of reactivity. We will be tested and tested again to reinforce our self-confidence, our worth, and our truth. We must remember that any person, no matter how reasonable-sounding, no matter how well we may think we know them, no matter what they say about themselves, no matter their credentials, if they undermine us, they are not to be trusted.

The good news is that even the rigid stance of the fearful masculine will self-destruct in time. We must remember it is not our job to fix or change anyone, but to simply allow their paroxysms of fear as we follow our own path. We remember, too, that given the limitless possibility of our own sovereignty, their path of fear has no real power to hurt us. It is best to disengage without explanation or apology and continue on, following the voice of your heart and staying open to those who are unconditionally loving and supportive.

The second general response to the revelation of oppression is for people, and men especially, to retreat into a place of shame. These men are often awake, sensitive, and loving, but they also live in constant apology for the very fact of their masculinity.

The prevailing model of masculinity has, historically, been one of dominance, competition, and oppression. As a result, the men in the second camp feel the brutality of this old model and believe their own manhood to be inherently tainted. These men are trying to atone for the wrongs of their forefathers by diminishing their power and vitality through self-effacement and shame. These men have effectively castrated themselves out fear of hurting others. They will often try to serve women, but beware- it often comes from a place of needing to be forgiven. These men need to be needed, seen, recognized, and praised for the "help" that they are giving.

There will be something sharp and unyielding in the awakened woman that has no patience for this hangdog gloominess. This shame-filled neediness is ultimately a form of self-obsession and not useful in any way to supporting her in her emerging role. She may have compassion for this man, but she cannot respect him, and she cannot ultimately trust him as an ally. He is in need of a mother to hold him, to let him know all will be ok, and that there's nothing wrong with him. He is also dangerous in the sense that, if he doesn't get what he needs from the woman, or if she makes it very clear that she doesn't need what he has to offer, he can become petulant and cruel, lashing out in childish rage, or getting lost in long, pedantic, and reasonable-sounding justifications for his weakness.

The awakened woman on the warpath of evolution simply does not have time for this. She cannot afford to stop and comfort the shameful little boy trying to atone for his sins. This man must learn to detach himself from the need to be needed and evolve beyond the self-obsession of his shame. A woman who coddles this man is acting from her own woundedness. She may try to help him, but deep down she will despise him.

Instead of recriminating herself for her "uncharitable" feelings, she should turn toward those feelings and listen. If she can learn to trust her feelings of contempt, disgust, and scorn without judgment of herself or the person eliciting the feelings, then she can allow these reactions to move her beyond her own need to be needed and liked. This frees her to step fully into her own power, which is desperately needed at this time. To put it bluntly, this transition period is a time of high stakes where women cannot waste time catering to the egos of wounded men.

There is a third camp of men, and I am glad to say it is growing in number (and will continue to do so rapidly as women refuse to use their energy in shoring up, soothing, and trying to "fix" the dysfunctional men in the first two camps). This dawning group of men have allowed and felt the depth of suffering, moved through shame, and are now emerging on the other side as creators of a new model of masculinity.

These men are authentically embracing the healed and sacred masculine. They emerge as living embodiments of an expression of pure masculinity that has nothing to do with power, competition, and dominance. Yet, their expression is unmistakably and undeniably *masculine*. These men understand that the greatest gift they can give women, and all of humanity is to allow masculinity itself to evolve through them into a new form. They do not apologize for their manhood, nor do they hide their vital, masculine power. Instead, they lead with their hearts and allow the expression of masculinity to move through them and into the world as a new, living model of manhood that has transcended into divine oneness.

There is a model of masculinity emerging on our planet that is quiet and present, decisive and strong, gentle and responsive, and always unconditionally loving. This is the final transmutation of the wounded masculine, the transformation of strength humbled (and thus amplified) in devotional service. This masculinity uses the power of the heart to harness clarity, alignment, sexual desire, and action into present and intentional creation. As these men place their unleashed love in service to the whole, we see perhaps to our surprise that they are holding the same sword as before- they are simply choosing to wield it differently.

I must end this section with a caution. If you are a man reading these words, and you are congratulating yourself on having attained this final, pure version of masculinity, I must inform you that you still have some work to do.

In the transcended state I just described, there is no process of self-congratulation or even self-reference. The framework of sacred masculinity I outlined would, in fact, be a bit bewildering to the man who has moved into that high and sacred realm. This is because he just *is*. He is no longer seeking, not from ignorance, fear, or resignation, but because he has finally stepped into the fullness and simplicity of his existence.

He is already complete and therefore needs no explanation or barometer to tell him who he is and what he is doing. Healed, whole, and surrendered, the sacred masculine is present in his very being, which emanates unmistakably through the totality of his existence.

For the men moving into this evolved state of masculinity, they just *know*. There is no need to explain it or justify it. They have given their hearts to the world and stepped into a transcendent state of oneness that expresses through their living body. Once this happens on a large scale for both men and women, it will be as though we transcended existence itself. Paradoxically, it is only then that we will truly begin to live.

Thriving

I would like to end this section on embodiment by describing the new goal of evolution, that is, thriving. As we resolve the age-old conflict between masculine and feminine, we define new, synchronistic roles for these energies that allow all energy to move fluidly through the body itself, without blockage or suppression.

Thriving, then, is something that happens through the body, and the communication of this thriving is reflected in the holistic and surrendered state of the person experiencing it. That is, it will be felt in the body and reflected through the expression of the subtle bodies- emotional, mental, and spiritual.

The body holds, in a single, dense point of existence, every dimension and aspect of reality that exists in the universe. The body, then, is our immediate gateway and unerring guide to the nature of reality. Souls incarnating into a human body hold a distinct advantage, as the body is the perfect teacher of consciousness. The body cannot help but reflect, perfectly, accurately, and without ambiguity, exactly the lessons needed in the moment to evolve.

In order to take full advantage of this superpower we must orient ourselves to the idea that the body is templated to live in perfect health. Beginning from this assumption, we can approach our own body as a researcher would, inquiring, without judgement, into the simple questions of what makes it feel good and what doesn't. We may find that some things we *think* feel good, such as addictions, actually result in discomfort or suffering.

The body is a holograph of Earth holding precisely her energy and power, yet our bodies will not be able to demonstrate the fullness of their gifts until they're allowed to thrive. This will require that we create conditions for thriving. A flower cannot expect to bloom in a snowstorm; an arctic fox cannot be expected to prosper in a desert. Likewise, we cannot hope to tap into the deep and miraculous nature of our bodies until we begin to live in a way that unconditionally supports its needs.

We may begin to notice and respond to our natural rhythms of sleep and wakefulness, of eating and movement. We may let these rhythms shift over time and with the seasons. In this way, we always have one inner ear turned toward the voice of the body, allowing it to tell us what it needs and when, allowing it to lead us into the perfect balance, health, and vitality that it is capable of achieving.

The lessons we learn and the fears we overcome as we allow our lives to come into harmony with the rhythms of our body will eventually crystalize into the wisdom we have to offer the world. It takes courage, after all, to prioritize the body. As mentioned earlier, our culture still views the body (and the Earth) as something to be conquered, overcome, denied, or forced into submission. The dominant way of life in our world layers artificial constructs over our lives, demanding that we live according to unnatural and arbitrary schedules. To decide, without question or compromise, that the body's needs are more important than an external agenda is a radical act of self-love.

I believe that tending to the body is the highest form of worship we can perform while living in human form. It is the most direct way for us to honor our Mother. Our bodies are one with the Earth herself, forming a perfect fractal of her majesty, magic, and wonder. As such, the lessons we learn through listening and responding to the needs of our body translate directly to the needs and solutions for healing and restoring Mother Earth. Our relationship then becomes symbiotic, reciprocal, and transpersonal as the Earth Mother responds to our growing courage by showing us the path to joyful thriving.

When we begin to tend to the body, the body itself will gradually begin to reveal its secrets to us- the secrets that led to the manifestation of the body in the first place. The body is a multidimensional instrument with the capacity to respond to unseen cosmic frequencies. It is a vast library holding access to all that has ever been known. We are hungry for this knowing, and it is time for the secrets of life to be revealed.

As the body reveals its secrets, we transform our view of evolution (both personal and collective) to be centered on thriving as opposed to simply survival. As mentioned before, "survival of the fittest" is the inevitable phrase we invoke when referring to evolution. However, embedded in the word "survival" lives the very presence of death itself. This means that death, an ever-present specter, has hitherto provided the tension for us to evolve. Mere survival is not, however, a place from which we can truly blossom, and we no longer need to invoke the fear of death in order to grow.

I don't believe many on Earth truly know what *thriving* really is. Many *think* they know what thriving is, but, other than rare glimpses, I don't believe many bodies on Earth have truly experienced it. It is in this arena of the New Earth (as with so many others) that we must release our mind's theoretical definition of thriving and allow our bodies to lead us into it. I believe that, once experienced, true thriving is unmistakable and unforgettable. Once the feeling of it has permeated our cells, then we have a point of reference, a standard by which to make our decisions.

Thriving occurs when we truly begin to live our most natural lives. A natural way of life will be deeply connected to the rhythms, cadence, and frequency of the Earth, as well as our own particular blend of joyful pursuits and responsiveness to the needs of the body.

The body, after all, has needs. I will say again, *the body has needs*. It is a finely-tuned instrument, an exquisite manifestation of divine artistry, and it has needs. We spend so much time denying, suppressing, or distracting ourselves from our true needs that many of us live disconnected from our bodies. We have become so numb that the only sensation strong enough to reach us is pain.

If your experience is anything like mine, once you turn toward your body and begin to truly listen with unconditional compassion to its voice, it is possible that you will feel the floodgates open. You may feel extraordinary rushes of feeling grief, rage, and shock. You may eventually feel the subtle aches and chronic tension that had been overshadowed by larger, more sweeping health issues. This is the pain, the grief, the rage, the shock, the tension and the aches that your body has experienced over the course of your lifetime but not been allowed to process or fully express.

When I finally chose to turn unconditionally toward my body, I was amazed the changes it demanded in the way I lived my life. After my first awakening, I slept for days (even now, during periods of integration, I still give in to immense exhaustion). Resting was new for me as I was always driven to be frantically up and about and *doing*. But I finally allowed myself to sleep as much as I needed without shame, anxiety, or judgment. As I rested, I felt a lifetime of grief, fear, anxiety, and judgement rise up to be seen, felt, and released. I trusted that my body would know how to move through the intensity, but I acknowledged that it required a lot of rest. This was a different kind of exhaustion than what I was accustomed to.

It was an astonishing thing for me to realize that, not only did I have needs, but that I was worthy of those needs being met. As I turned inward to the voice of my body, we began building a relationship together founded on trust, listening, and love. My body started to understand that its voice would be acknowledged and acted upon. As a result, like any relationship, it began opening to me, telling me more and more about itself. It told me the reasons for my addictions, compulsions, and longings. It let me see to the root of my desires. As I touched on the origin of these things, I became increasingly able to forgive myself for my past choices.

As we continue to evolve our relationship, I believe that my body will begin showing me even deeper secrets: secrets of thriving, of creation, and of magic. These revelations cannot, however, be rushed. The body must simply be met, moment to moment, whisper by whisper, one day at a time.

It was a courageous commitment to choose to meet the needs of my body no matter how "unreasonable," "inconvenient," or "expensive." However, once I began to act in accord with my newfound sense of worthiness, I was astonished to see how the universe gathered to support me. Miracles come to me. I have learned to open and receive them, not through a sense of entitlement, but from a feeling of worthiness, gratitude, and devotion. I let the universe worship me as I have begun to worship myself- not, as the ego would, through vanity and pride, but as God would, through joy and love, tenderness, and unconditional support. I began to worship myself as a divine creation, as a holy temple of God's light. In doing so, I show the world how I expect- and deserve- to be treated.

Someday we will transcend our physical needs. However, I have learned that this type of magic cannot be forced. No need can be transcended until it has been fully met.

The path to thriving, then, begins with meeting your body with compassion in every given moment. When you prioritize meeting the needs of your body, it will relax more and more into trust. As the body relaxes into trust, your whole being begins to relax into trust, and as with any relationship, a deepening of trust engenders a deepening of intimacy. Your body will gradually begin to open, to blossom, and to reveal long-held secrets, powers, and miracles that have for so long been hidden by fear.

As we embrace our bodies as the perfect, divine expression of our soul, our evolution will expand and accelerate immeasurably as it becomes driven, no longer by fear of death, but by a genuine and joyful love of life.

Original Sin, Debt, and Redemption

I turn now to a contemplation on the force that broke humans apart from God. In this section I examine the driving pressure that shame exerts on humans, both individually and as a collective. My intention is to unpick the dark threads of our human tapestry, winding back to the origin of shame in order to unravel the subtle and pernicious hold it has over us. We can then start again from the beginning, weaving a tapestry where those dark threads have been transmuted into something precious.

I attest here that shame has been so deeply imprinted and reinforced into our psyche that we've mistaken it for our very nature. Shame is a compelling and powerful force, but ultimately, as we will see, it is fragile when brought into the light of loving awareness.

--

Since the moment "of man's first disobedience," humans have acted under the illusion that we are a tainted race: separate, cast off, and irredeemable except through excruciating methods of atonement. The stories of our inherent unworthiness, perpetuated by many religions, have permeated the very beliefs on which we've built our lives and global systems. However, we cannot lay blame (so to speak) at the feet of religious institutions, which simply reflect and amplify a frequency that already existed on our planet before they- the institutions- were ever constructed. Shame existed as a nameless feeling, a frequency, an image, an archetype far before it was gathered and expressed through a sophisticated narrative arc. Because shame is a primordial and undifferentiated force that burst into being at the very moment of our conscious awakening, humans assumed, excusably, it must have always been an undeniable aspect of our nature. From that assumption we wove a tight and constricting fabrication that reinforced the stories of our innate unworthiness. We have repeated these stories so many times, and in so many ways, that they have taken on the insidious guise of fact.

This is the origin, so to speak of "original sin." The stories of our inherent unworthiness, which are reinforced both overtly and implicitly, affect every human on Earth whether or not a person has ever even set foot in a place of worship. We have breathed into our very bodies the belief that we are somehow innately ugly and deformed, separate from the Earth, from the divine, and from each other. I have heard humans described, by other humans, as "bad, evil, diseased, a cancer on this planet… the Earth would be better off without us." Perhaps these beliefs run, even ever so subtly, through your own subconscious.

In response to a belief in our "original sin," humans have plunged themselves into a vague and bewildering purgatory where the sweet relief of redemption lies in the hands of a capricious, faceless, punishing, and remote God-figure. No matter how hard we try to atone for the past, there is always more to be done. We climb an endless mountain of shame and guilt, never reaching the top and never being allowed to rest. Redemption, then, becomes a moving and arbitrary target where we exhaust ourselves ad infinitum through labor and suffering, wondering how much pain we will be forced to endure before we are finally allowed back home.

Ultimately, this scenario describes what it means to be in debt. We believe we have fallen from grace through our own willfulness, and we must earn, through an undisclosed amount of misery and pain, our way back into the conceptual and remote realm of heaven. Furthermore, it is only the relentless force of shame that can offer us redemption, as shame itself offers the only known provocation for us to pay off our spiritual debt- causing us to do something (i.e., suffer greatly) in order to prove ourselves worthy of existing. So, we cling to shame as our only salvation from the very predicament in which shame has placed us.

It is important to note that all manifested forms originate first within the consciousness of self. Therefore, the life we live is a perfect representation of our personal beliefs. As every human is an encapsulated fractal of the whole, the entire world is therefore a simple projection of our collective beliefs. Through the law of sovereign free will, all frequencies that we harbor must somehow take shape in the external world. When viewed this way, we can learn much about ourselves by examining the external world as a mirror of our internal personal and collective beliefs.

Because of this law of free-will manifestation, the debt we feel within- that dark, dogged chasm of unworthiness and shame- has inevitably projected itself onto our manifested world as monetary debt. Debt has, in fact, become the major arbiter of our lives, hanging over us like a dense and heavy cloud. As I write this, our global "debt" sits at a record amount, in the hundreds of trillions of dollars. We can see how the frequency of spiritual debt that has for so long blindly driven us into greater and greater states of suffering has manifested as a mirror in our global economics.[14] The good news is that, while seemingly intractable, these debts are in truth nothing more than belief figments and can be changed literally overnight if we so choose.

Debt consciousness is the ultimate result of our belief in what we refer to as "original sin," (the belief that we have committed an irredeemable act of willfulness and therefore owe an undisclosed

---

[14] It would be a fascinating study to use this understanding as a lens to examine the complex movement of global debt. Shame and resentment are the same frequency expressed in different ways, as such I would posit that the nations most in debt to others are the ones that hold the deepest levels of hidden resentment. For instance, if Country A is, of all the nations, most in debt to Country B, we may hypothesize that Country A harbors deep, unspoken, and unresolved resentment and anger toward Country B, an energy which is reflected in their financial relationship. Forgiveness is, of course, the only way to move past debt, as we will see.

amount of suffering and misery to God in order to be saved), and an inquiry into debt consciousness- that is, a willingness to embrace debt as a spiritual teacher- actually offers us the clearest and most direct pathway to our ultimate redemption.

Let's begin by examining the word "sin." I believe the key to understanding this word lives within its very meaning. In the Spanish language, *sin* means, "without," (in Latin, the word is *sine*). Sin, then, as I define it, simply means to act *without* conscious invocation of the divine. A sinful action is one undertaken *without* conscious deference to the eternal and abiding energy and presence of the divine. Therefore, when we act "in sin," it simply means we have forgotten to infuse our choices and creations with divine energy. "Sin" then cannot be resolved through judgment or shame. It simply refers to a lack of presence.

It remains a law of Earth that any choice, action, or creation cannot help but perpetuate the state of consciousness of the one who has undertaken the choice, action, or creation. When we act with conscious presence, when we bring divine awareness in our choices, we automatically perpetuate divine will. Acting "in sin" means simply that we have forgotten our antecedents and thus heedlessly perpetuate the consciousness of debt.

The root of debt is the ego, which is the concentrated force of separation. The solitary ego, and the debt that it perpetuates, holds no inherent life force of its own. It is thus inherently parasitic. Ego and debt cannot survive as separate entities unless infused with massive amounts of external life force from a host. Any creation emerging from the ego is not imbued independently with light but must, like a parasite, draw life force from its creator and all who come in contact with it.[15]

---

[15] In this way, the manifested, Earthly parasite is a living representation of debt- it is an entity that takes and takes and takes, that never gives back, that is never satiated, and that offers no benefit whatsoever to its host.

Original *sin*, then, was that first moment of trauma in which humans believed themselves to be *without* God. We found ourselves in pain, seemingly abandoned, and we turned toward the ego for our salvation. The fact of the trauma itself seemed a communication of our inherent unworthiness. We believed we were separate from the divine and therefore beyond redemption.

From that moment forward we lived "in sin," that is *without* a belief in our own inherent divinity. This gave rise to shame, blame, and recrimination, which was pointed both inwards and toward those we saw in the world. As sovereign creators living in a collective agony of shame, we could not help but project that shame into the manifested world. As a result, our collective systems amplify the belief that we are innately unworthy, alone, and existing in a perpetual and irredeemable state of debt.

Put very simply, debt consciousness is the belief that there is something we must still do to make ourselves worthy, whole, and complete. Under these auspices, humans live constantly on trial, trying exhaustively to prove ourselves worthy. We try to prove ourselves in different ways: through what we produce, through suffering and sacrifice, through worry and micro-managing, through how busy we can become, through making ourselves into victims. Overall, in the larger system of debt and proving, some humans are deemed worthy (of food, shelter, love, health, safety, warmth, joy) while others are not. Those that have proven themselves worthy are acclaimed; those that have shown themselves to be unworthy are generally judged, cast off, and blamed.

The illusion that we are somehow separate from divine life force, or that there is something we must do to "get it," gives rise to the fear that energy, resources, life, and love itself is somehow limited. This caused us to strike out as best we could, creating hierarchies and imposing artificial systems of order, which has in turn resulted in the ravening, hungry-hungry-hippo mentality toward our commons of our Earth. If the source of love is not within us, it must be outside of us. If it is outside of us, then it can be taken, ergo, we must protect it fiercely. And so, we live like clay pots with holes in the bottom, never filled, never nourished, never satiated, taking from the Earth and from each other in an ongoing desperate attempt to replenish the bottomless, empty void that was left when God abandoned us.

    We can be pardoned for believing that energy is limited, as that is how it *feels* to live within systems that have sprung from debt consciousness. As mentioned before, "sinful" systems hold no life force of their own, so to maintain them we must drain our own life force in service to them. This is similar to how parasites act within the body. Also like parasites, as we will see, once we remove our energy and life force from these systems and beliefs, they naturally die their own deaths.

    So, we have touched on the essence of redemption. The answer to our redemption lies in our willingness to remove our energy from that which does not hold its own life force. We do this in our lives by kindly-but-firmly saying "no" to that which does not serve us. Internally, this process culminates in an unwillingness to harbor any thought, feeling, or emotion that does not uphold the inherent worthiness and divinity of all beings.

    Descartes' influential statement "*Cogito, ergo sum*," ("I think, therefore I am,") offers a subtle (and may I add, masculine) reflection of our pervasive belief in separation. With this statement, Descartes has assumed that we realize existence through the mind. We see ourselves as the effect of the mind; as such we elevate thought as the necessary precursor to being. We have, in effect, thunk ourselves into existence.[16] Creation through the mind of the small "i" always results in a sliver of separation between who we are in truth and who we *think* we are. In this way, who we *think* we are is an illusion that nevertheless becomes our reality.

In contrast, the mantra of the New Earth will be the simple and profound tautology, "I am, therefore I AM." Our very bodies, as a perfect expression of our souls, is proof of our divinity. This is true, without exception, for every being, animal, plant, mineral, human, on our planet. All are perfect manifestations of grace.

We start, then, with the premise, not that we are inherently tainted, but that all beings on this planet are, by virtue of their very existence, a holy manifestation of divine will. Therefore, while there are diverse differences in expression, there is no gradation of worthiness. Divine law is unconditional love, absent of judgment, criticism, blame, manipulation, and hierarchy. It is pure and purely free. These are the laws that amplify, rather than drain, life force. These are the laws on which we will build our new world. It is through embracing these laws that the New Eden will manifest as Earth herself. Once we allow ourselves to be lifted into divine law, every place and every being on Earth will become paradise. We cannot make a "wrong" decision because we ourselves will be aligned with divine will. Therefore, our every action cannot help but perpetuate divinity. Everywhere we go, and with everything we do, we will encounter only that which is life-giving, nourishing, and supportive. All will be reclaimed into love. As this Eden dawns, we enter into the divine and effortless ecstasy of being.

Divine law is extremely challenging to the mind and ego, which endlessly seek rationalization and justification for our choices.

---

[16] This is actually true at the level of the higher mind, but that mind would never use the phrase "I think," because within the higher mind there is no "I" to speak of. As well, in this realm, thought is not separate from will.

We weigh the rightness of our decisions in the balance of the external world, placing ourselves against some abstract barometer of worthiness.

In this place of confusion, it is important to know that we have, literally at our fingertips, the compass, map, and guide back to our own divine nature. I refer to the Earth herself, and indeed our very bodies, which exist as an immaculate conception of perfect grace.

The Earth is a perfect fractal of the Universe, and our bodies are a perfect fractals of the Earth. Therefore, all we need to know about the nature of existence lives immediately within us and around us in the natural world. Turning to our bodies and our Earth as teachers will help us discern between what is divine law and what is "sin," that is, the human laws, dictates, and influences that were created *without* divine presence and are therefore illusory.

As we turn to our bodies and the Earth as our teachers, one thing we will learn immediately is that debt does not actually exist anywhere in the manifested realm. In the simplest terms, existence is comprised of two aspects. There is form and there is nothingness- the binary of one and zero. There is no manifested "negative." The "lowest" we can go in existence is zero- the space of pure void, the unfathomable "no-thing."

Therefore, we can see that debt itself is a purely theoretical invention. It only exists so long as we persist in believing in it. As such, the very notion of debt (along with other theoretical inventions of judgement, blame, criticism, and manipulation) will be released naturally over time as we reclaim our energy and turn instead toward that which is life-giving. Debt, judgment, blame, criticism, and manipulation are all "sinful," energies that is, *without* independent life force, and are therefore parasitic in nature. As we release these beliefs, we will reclaim a massive amount of life force for ourselves individually, and for humanity as a whole. We will be astounded at how much energy we have been channeling to keep these entities alive, and we will be amazed at the amount of energy we have available to us when we are free of them.

The release of all debt on the planet allows us to reframe the concept and process of redemption. From the divine perspective, of course, there is no need for redemption, as we have never actually been separate from God. From our human perspective, however, as we travel the road from illusory separation to Unity consciousness, it helps to have a pathway that we can trust. This is the ultimate pathway to redemption, that is, our final and irreversible lifting beyond debt, beyond sin, and into peace.

This pathway to redemption is formed by the three human inventions that are perfectly aligned with divine will. These, as we mentioned already, are the trinity of compassion, discernment, and forgiveness. This trinity forms the technology of our salvation. Ultimately these too will be released as we merge into our truest nature. Until then, however, they serve as useful tools for guiding us on our ascension.

We employ discernment to distinguish between that which is life-giving and that which is not. As we become progressively more discerning, choosing only to allow into our lives that which is holy, the theoretical inventions of humanity- those concepts that were conceived "in sin" - will naturally dissolve.

When we employ compassion, we can see the underlying structures and the larger forces that motivate actions we would judge as "bad" or harmful." When we tune inwards, we see that all of the "bad" or "harmful" impulses of humanity are simply impersonal frequencies filtered through the complex inheritance of our wounds. As we accept these impulses, confront the ways in which they affect us, and explore their origins, we come to understand that at the root of all things, even the worst acts we can imagine, is only love. As we understand and love ourselves through the lifting of our shadows, understand that self-love is the key to understanding and forgiving all of humanity.

The more we understand ourselves, the easier it is to forgive and release that which we carry. In practicing forgiveness, we slowly erode our ego and become transparent, dropping the heavy frequencies of resentment, righteousness, anger, fear, and victimhood.

At some point, as we go about our life practicing discernment, compassion, and forgiveness, we reach such a state of radiance and transparency that redemption happens automatically and, perhaps, unexpectedly. It is not something we need to "do," "accomplish," or "achieve." It is almost as if, having dropped all that is heavy, we have shrunk the gap of illusory separation to such a degree that grace can easily do the rest, gleefully scooping us up into a new state of being, one in which we have dissolved completely and are thus indistinguishable from grace itself.

In this state of being, every aspect of our lives resonates, naturally and effortlessly, in harmony with divine will. We remain present to the divine in all moments, and so "sin" melts away into something that has never been, and God comes to rest within us. Every action, every word, every movement, every gesture is, naturally and effortlessly, a form of worship, and we cannot help but spread love wherever we go. In this state of being, "what we do" is unimportant, as our very breath infuses light into the world. The state of redemption confers unparalleled freedom, as any and every one of our creations is conceived immaculately within us. We become prayer embodied, moving through the world as beacons of divine light.

Atonement

As we come to consciously embody the energy of the New Eden, we will finally acknowledge that there is no such thing as the compartmentalization of our lives. Indeed, we will realize that the possibility of "compartmentalization" was only ever an artificial mental structure that became layered over the reality of our true nature. We live, lead, and act, work, labor, breathe, and love, inevitably, with the totality of our being. This is always true, and the extent to which we resist this truth will define a large portion of our daily suffering.

The New Eden is a place of unremitting transparency. The current Earth, in fact, is also one of absolute transparency if we choose to approach it in this way. When we allow ourselves to remain open and surrendered, we can see how the entire world conspires to unearth the things we have been trying desperately to hide.

Any part of your being that you have denied, hidden, or tucked away will emerge one way or another in your life in order to bring to light the aspects of yourself that you cannot accept. The parts that remain cloaked in shadow will become apparent in your business, the people you hire, the people you work with, the partners you choose, your children, and the situations that rise up around you. In the time of the Great Change, nothing will be allowed to remain hidden. All will be brought into the light for revelation, healing and finally, acceptance. In the end, you will be left with nothing but the truth of your being. This is your deepest essence, and it comes from the reclamation of your entire self- nothing hidden, and nothing denied. Such is the process of atonement.

We have hidden from the prospect of atonement because, in the long, dark era of separation we were accustomed to being manipulated and controlled through shame. It was not safe to offer to the light aspects of ourselves that would inevitably be condemned.

Under the penetrating eye of that Whom we categorized as a cruel and ruthless Father God- the one that cast Adam and Eve from the garden and cursed them to endless toil and suffering- the path to atonement was painted as arduous, thankless, exhausting, and never-ending. The ultimate coup of the ego was when we internalized this shame and, without even the need of external reinforcement, began cloaking our own power in shadow so as not to bear witness to our unbridled divinity.

In the dawning era we will come to understand that this God - the harsh, judgmental arbiter of right and wrong - was only ever a figment, a figure born from fear, suffering and the need to displace our own limitless power. He was a creation of the dark belief that we are somehow separate from God and must prove ourselves worthy of His love- a love He withholds if we do not measure up.

The divine force in our new era demonstrates how shame, and all of the trappings of shame, are an illusion. We realize Eden within us when we uphold the truth of our divinity, our core goodness, and our innate, unconditional worthiness. This state of unity and love has always been and always will be- it was only our fears that obscured its eternal presence within us.

Atonement asks you to unearth every aspect of self that you have suppressed, denied, or kept hidden. It is a full reclamation of self, the resolute re-membering of your whole being. At this point in our evolution, when the New Earth has not yet been fully established, atonement is a courageous and mythic adventure as it requires us to step boldly through the veils of our own making. Ultimately, atonement is inseparable from our inner Eden. As we take into our arms the totality of self, we will discover that Eden is inside of us. That in fact, it *is* us, but it can only manifest when it is (we are) complete, whole, and uncloaked.

We begin with the premise that you were created flawless. There is not one part of you that is extraneous or a mistake. Another way to think of this is to assume that you were designed to exactly and precisely fulfill the purpose for which you were born. This purpose is the emanation of your own unique and irreplaceable genius. However, you cannot fulfil your purpose if even one tiny speck of you remains hidden from view.

The very word "atonement" offers a clue as to its nature. Atonement (at-ONE-ment) means to be fully at one, or in perfect unity, with yourself. As you reclaim hidden aspects of self and place them in service to your higher purpose, you will find that they knit themselves into the unified nature of your own sovereignty, bringing you truly into a state of perfect, undifferentiated wholeness.

In China, there are healing practitioners known as bonesetters. Mastery of this art involves the painstaking reconstruction of a shattered bone, with the healer replacing even the most minute shards into perfect placement. These healers are able to do this without cutting open the skin. With their inner sight they are able to see the bone, the bone shards, and the entire process of reconstruction clearly without the use of anything but their own hands.

Imagine, for a moment, the process of atonement as being similar to the action of the bonesetter. The bonesetter is your higher self, but instead of reconstructing bone, it reconstructs your soul, piecing together the shards that had fragmented away through shame, shock, and trauma. You may imagine that each fragment of self is the shape of a sacred geometric form, and when placed together, the seams of your reconstructed self formed stunning patterns of sacred geometry.

As you reach atonement, that is, at the moment when all fragments of self are recovered and set delicately into their rightful place, you may feel waves of unimaginable energy expanding outward from where the fragments are touching. At the moment of atonement, your being becomes a kintsugi masterpiece, with golden light shining from every juncture.

Surrender

The vast majority of humans have not, in their conscious awareness, been exposed to the frequency of unconditional compassion. Though some of us have felt it as infants, most of us, after reaching the conscious, self-referential stage of development, have only ever experienced a conditional form of love.

Many people *think* they know what unconditional love feels like, but, like all enlightened frequencies, it is not something that can be thought about- it must be consciously experienced in the body itself. If you have felt it, you know it intrinsically. If you're not certain, it hasn't happened yet. If you *think* you're certain, it hasn't happened yet.

Every person has the capacity to feel and offer unconditional love and compassion. It is the natural, intrinsic, and unchanging nature of the heart. As our heart exists already in an enduring and eternal state of unconditional love, it can easily demonstrate this love to our conscious awareness. This requires, however, openness and a humble willingness to receive.

It also requires courage. Many of us have been wounded by fear masquerading as love. As children we may have been scolded, judged, beaten, violated, insulted, or yelled at in the name of love. "I am only angry because I love you; I am only punishing you because I love you," are, perhaps, ways we were mis-taught about the nature of love. This form of "love" was extremely painful, and we understandably became very wary about opening to receive more. Our misconceptions about love may have manifested later in life as we experienced intimacy and vulnerability with friends, partners, and children. We would perpetuate the patterns that we were taught was love. As a result, many of us may grow weary, cynical, and full of rage at the exhortation to simply "surrender into love." In our experience, surrendering to "love" was an agonizing experience, and one we do not care to repeat.

Anger, judgement, violation, anxiety, blame, criticism, violence, manipulation, gaslighting, lying, stonewalling, trespassing on clearly-established boundaries, and all other forms of abuse in any form from any person are *not* examples of love. Accepting and surrendering to these things is *not an act of love*, and it is *not required* in order to reach your highest expression. True love will never ask you to abase, demean, betray, or diminish yourself. True love is only ever empowering.

So how can we learn to surrender into actual love, especially if we have not consciously experienced it? For this, I turn to the archetype of the slave. This incredible archetype offers powerful guidance on the alchemical nature of divine surrender. The slave shows deeply the way of surrender, having given over his or her life, will, and freedom over to another. When we work with this archetype, we learn how to enact surrender as a form of worship.

The slave becomes a shadowed archetype when its devotional surrender is co-opted in service to the ego. Many of us have experienced this type of exploitation- in relationships, in our workplaces- where our talents, skills, and the light of our heart us used for gain, profit, and/or the personal gratification of another without offering energy or love back in return. This situation is further compounded when the enacted model then turns on us, blaming us for our fatigue and lifting it up as an example of our lack of resilience or dedication. We think there must be something wrong with us, and if we can simply try harder, give more, or love with more fervor then all will be solved. But of course, it never does, and it never is. In a model such as this, the more we give, the more it is taken. We become depleted, resentful, and reluctant to give more.

As a result, many of us have shut down the possibility of full and unfettered self- expression. We have hidden our greatest gifts because, when they emerge, they are harvested by forces that do not appreciate the light, grace, mastery, and beauty inherent in the offering. As a result, our most prominent model of surrender is toxic. So, we resist surrender desperately and hide our deepest strengths under so many layers of fear that not even *we* can access them. They remain a secret even to us.

The slave archetype teaches us that sacrifice in and of itself is not a virtue. When we sacrifice our wellbeing, when we compromise our dignity and power for something that is small and unworthy, we are not committing an act of grace but perpetuating a cycle of abuse.

We become what we surrender to, so when we follow the highest instinct of the slave archetype, which is guided by the light of the heart, we will naturally surrender only to that which amplifies our strength, dignity, and grace. The heart always leads back toward itself, so this continued conscious surrender will bring us inevitably into the space of unconditional love. With unerring instinct, the heart will let you know whether or not you are being confronted with authentic, sincere, open and earnest truth, or with something that is untrustworthy, conditional, and inauthentic. As you choose to let your heart lead beyond logic and reason and toward refined frequencies of light, you will eventually anchor a deep and natural knowledge of love within you.

Ultimately, the slave archetype teaches us the path to atonement. It shows us how to work with the energy of surrender so that we become increasingly empowered. When we learn to surrender to *only* the highest light of our heart something miraculous happens: we are reborn into the light, *as* the light. In this way, the slave shows us how we can travel alchemically from the "lowest" and "least-empowered" aspect of self and, through the intelligence of surrendering only to that which empowers us, eventually become

God. This is the ultimate form of atonement: to become "at one" with the very essence of divinity.

Unconditional Love

With breathtaking presumption I will now endeavor to relay the essence of unconditional love. I humbly admit to the inadequacy of my words and can only hope that a tendril of this incredible force is present within the transmission.

I want to approach my description by underlining what unconditional love is and what it is *not*. It is imperative, as we move forward in the new era of consciousness, to illuminate misconceptions about unconditional love, as I have seen so many deny, betray, and silence themselves in an effort to only project that which they believe is acceptable, loving, and harmless. I assure you, Reader, that if you are denying, suppressing, or silencing a deep truth, you are perpetuating more harm than you can imagine.

It can be a disorienting experience to consciously embody unconditional love. It is not what we "think" it is, and, in the early stages of its dawning, it can be easily misconstrued and trespassed upon if we do not use it to establish boundaries. Boundaries, as we will see, are in no way anathema to either unconditional love or unity consciousness. They are absolutely necessary to our ability to thrive.

How to set clear boundaries was my own personal deepest lesson of unconditional love. After the experience of having my heart opened,[17] I spent a long time wandering in the proverbial desert, offering my love to places, people, and situations that were, I understand now, unworthy of it. I believed that unconditional love meant that I had no right to feel, let alone express, the seemingly "unloving" emotions that rose in me, including rage and disgust. I no

---

[17] an experience that continues, like the "widening gyre," to deepen in experience, breadth, and intensity far beyond the realm of my control. Much of this is captured in my memoir, *Finding Home*.

longer held a template for cruelty, brutality, exploitation, or abuse, so I was confused by many of the responses people had toward me. My love was at times co-opted, sexualized, and exploited by others. In these situations, I was uncertain as to how to respond except with more love and more giving. I thought I must not be loving enough or giving enough if others were dissatisfied. Wasn't that the meaning of unconditional love? To give and give and never expect anything in return?

It took me quite some time, and much confusion, violation, and heartbreak, to understand that the most effective and powerful application of unconditional love is to direct it first inward, toward the self. Once I embraced the belief that I was unconditionally worthy of fulfillment, once I began tending *first* to *my* needs, *my* health, and *my* wellbeing, deep processes of transformation began to detonate in my body. My life became simpler, easier, and, while still intense, it was more directed, streamlined, and fulfilling. My health and vitality began stabilizing. Resources and helpful, loving people began flowing into my life.

Through learning to love myself without condition, I began to show myself -and thus those around me- the standard to which I expected to be treated. I learned there is a big difference between self-love and selfishness, between clear and honest self-advocacy and narcissism. I began practicing a mantra which, to this day, is one of my favorites. It is very simple and direct. It is, "no thank you." With this mantra I began to practice active discernment in all aspects of my life, ruthlessly clearing that which no longer supported me and my purpose, giving myself everything I needed regardless of "practicality," and absolutely refusing, under any circumstances, to compromise my wellbeing, safety, emotional needs, or values. In taking this stand, the world rallied to support me, often in astonishing ways.

As I practiced rigorous discernment, I discovered that honest and unapologetic self-advocacy is not welcomed by everyone. I am not always liked. Standing in my truth would quite often result in backlash and subtle sharp prods of blame or criticism. I accepted these reactions and used them as reflections on my choices. I asked myself honestly if I had been acting from self-love or ego. I examined my intentions and motives. I came to the conclusion that if I could truly declare that my decision had come from self-love, and it was not welcomed by someone else, then that person must have their own agenda that had nothing to do with my wellbeing. This was especially reinforced if the other person reacted with subtle (or overt) shaming, blame, and self-justification.

I treated these moments as tests. To my delight, I learned that "being liked" is not my highest aspiration in life. Nor, if I am frank, do I "like" everyone I meet, though my practice has become to unconditionally respect their paths and choices. When I operate by the values of integrity, honesty, compassion, and self-love, when I say "yes," and mean it, and "no," and mean it, those who are supportive and loving will naturally remain, and those who are not will inevitably leave my sphere. I operate from the assumption that I am always and eternally forgiven. This means I owe nothing to anyone, and all I offer is freely given from a place of centeredness and sovereignty.

Over time, I began to unpiece the conflations within my psyche- between self-worth and entitlement, between confidence and arrogance, between sovereignty and selfishness. Over and above, I trusted the voice of my heart. If it did not open to a person, situation, conversation, or opportunity, I listened. I let it guide me even when it pointed directly opposite to the "logic" or "appearance" of a situation.

From a place of wellbeing and trust, I can brim over with confidence, love, and joy for those around me without fear of compromising myself. I know myself well enough to say "no," without apology or explanation, to any person, situation, or contract that doesn't serve my highest purpose.

I still receive the bright and multi-chromatic spectrum of emotions that shiver through all of humanity. I am learning to trust these emotions as signals. As I move through life, I watch myself as though through the eyes of loving, divine parents. If I become fussy, irritable, or frustrated, it is a sign that there is a need I am not meeting for myself. So, I withdraw, approach the feeling with compassionate inquiry, and tend to my needs before doing anything else. I set loving intentions for my life and follow through, not with force, but with resolve, surrender, and firmness.

It feels as though, after a lifetime of expending the power of my love on others, I am finally gathering these resources into the deep, calm reservoir of my own being. I am discovering an innate ability to care for and nourish all of my bodies, and the capacity to create calm, serene, orderly sanctuaries around me. For the first time in my life, I have decided to turn my nurturing power fully inward, toward the self. As I receive my own gifts, I begin to understand, for the first time, their incredible value and potency. I resolve to only offer these gifts to those who can appreciate their worth.

There is a story of Lakshmi, the Hindu Goddess of abundant life-force, generosity, and fecundity, that taught me much about the natural movement of love, tenderness, and joy.

At one time Vishnu, the consort of Lakshmi, was cruel and indifferent to her. Immediately, Lakshmi disappeared. She left him and dove deep into the ocean where he could not follow.

Without her, the crops withered. The animals died. A heavy shroud of weariness and depression fell over the land and its people as their life force slowly ebbed away. The people begged Vishnu to make amends with Lakshmi, to bring her back and renew their land and spirits.

Finally, Vishnu, humbled and moved by the suffering of his land, his people, and his own self, went to the water's edge and fell to his knees. He repented and begged Lakshmi to come back to him. She heard his sincere remorse and rose, like Venus, from the ocean waves.

When we follow the rhythms illuminated in this story, we move with the cosmic order of things even if it may seem, on the surface, like conflict. Joy and brightness and innocence cannot live when subjected to harshness, cruelty, indifference, and judgment. The feminine life force must be nurtured and revered, loved and respected. If it is not, it disappears. When we are subjected to people who approach us with cruelty and judgment, we must know that our life force cannot sustain itself in their presence. We do not owe them our light or our love. If we do not draw boundaries, if we do not move away from their harshness, we will watch our own joy recede to somewhere dark and unfathomable.

You will notice Lakshmi did not try to reason with Vishnu. She didn't try and talk to him of her feelings and her needs; she didn't seek out a mediator. Such is not the natural way of things. The vibrant life force of the feminine flows naturally toward that which is open and receptive, gentle and loving, and it flows away from that which is harsh and unfeeling. Unconditional love means that we allow our energy to move toward that which naturally honors and amplifies our life force.

So often, in our desire to nurture, to love, and to connect we take on the burden of other people's choices. Such is not the way of unconditional self-love, nor is it the way of sovereignty. We are under no obligation to pour our precious life force into people, situations, and commitments that do not hold, revere, and honor our light. We let others make their choices, and we are free to make our own choices in return, without rancor, resentment, or the need to fix, change, or save anyone. We speak our truth, and we let it be. As we allow things to be, and as we allow others their choices without attachment, we remain, as did Lakshmi, a loving and receptive space should they ever wish to *humbly and sincerely* return to us. However, our wellbeing does not depend on such an outcome.

This lesson, the letting go of other people's burdens, is an ongoing practice for me. I have to remind myself that taking on the burdens of others is not an expression of unconditional love but a trespass on their sovereignty. I can give the light that wishes to flow to them; I can offer compassion and love if it is a life-giving and generative act, but my first responsibility must be always to myself, my light, and my truth.

It is true that the soul doesn't have aversions. However, there are truths that enliven and generate life, and there are situations that draw life force away. My body and my life are temples of unimaginable beauty, and I am allowed to choose unilaterally who and what has access to these temples.

I am learning to embrace Lakshmi in all of her love and abundance, joy, gentleness and generosity. I am watching where she flows, whom she opens to, when she retreats. I trust her movement and follow it with my life.

In my commitment to this work, I continually bring into balance these sacred masculine and feminine energies that form the bedrock of all immaculate creation. As this occurs within, I become a living embodiment of the holy trinity. My feminine aspect expresses through life-force and creativity, abundance, emotion, movement, a delight in the senses, nurturing, wonder, and tenderness. My masculine expresses through protection and clarity, spaciousness, simplicity, honesty, confidence, structure, and devotion. As these forces harmonize within me, the neutral aspect, the child, is born through my life in all that I create and all that I am.

With the holy trinity balanced within, I live, speak, and create from a place of fearlessness, dignity, love, and wholeness. I am totally free, unencumbered, unbound, and unafraid. My life becomes a prayer of movement and creation. I give that which emanates from my deepest center- nothing more, and nothing less. In this way, my very being becomes my gift to the world, untouched and uninfluenced by the judgment of others. Such is freedom. Such is joy. Such is unconditional love.

The Power of the Heart

It is a quaking thing, to feel the infinite move through the finite medium of our bodies. When we open to it, we find, not that nothing matters, but everything matters so much that we cannot hope to ever contain it. In the vast presence of our own relentless light, we are broken open. This is crucifixion- to finally surrender to the shattering cosmic power of holding love in a body that can only live and breathe and walk for this short while. To love deeply that which will someday be gone is the unbearable ache of our existence. It is the threshold of tenderness, the final turning toward that which matters above all else.

In a culture that denies death we tend to forget that which is truly precious to us. We spend our time trying to elude, outwit, and outmaneuver death instead of allowing it to guide us toward those things that it cannot touch. Death will come, but in this moment it cannot take away the sun on my face, the river rushing below my feet, the songbird flitting like joy in the branches of the oak. Death holds tenderly a container for all that is fleeting in the human experience. In the face of that cosmic truth, our fears seem very small and very far away indeed.

When we truly contemplate death, we begin to turn towards that which we can see, feel, touch. We break open into a flourishing explosion of light so vast it cannot be contained or directed- toward "that" person or "that" thing. We become like the sun itself, shining the burning countenance of our love onto all that we meet.

In a culture that defines love as exclusive, channeled only through specific relationships and, largely, sexual urges, feeling this overwhelming tenderness toward all beings can be at first bewildering. Perhaps it is even more bewildering to those who encounter it, thinking somehow that the emanating love they receive is personal. Many- those who have not yet uncovered their own taproot to source- will want instinctively to co-opt, control, contain, or claim the person offering this love, like a freezing person trying to possess fire. This is the basis of many abusive and co-dependent relationships, with one person fearing desperately that, if the other person leaves, all of their light, love, and warmth will disappear as well.

As you merge with the radiance of your heart's universal grace, expect to attract those who are starving, cold, lonely, and lost as well as those who are humble, open, and surrendered. Calibrating to universal love will require firm discernment, as not all in the world is ready to amplify your light. It is necessary to define boundaries alongside the infinite love that blossoms eternally from your center. Yet, even in the midst of your boundaries, you do not stop loving them, even if you turn them from your door.

To command in a finite body the infinite power of love for creation and transmutation, we must learn to simultaneously penetrate and surrender to the mystery of our heart. In our culture the heart, as with many other sources of feminine power, has been largely denigrated as weak. The heart is considered "warm and fuzzy," cute, and nice, but it isn't practical when there's actual work to be done. The heart is all too often the first thing to be relinquished in times of pressure and fear. At those times we place our faith instead in rigidity and worry, intensifying our response and leaning heavily on that which has never worked in the past. As a result, we compromise our deepest nature to forcibly achieve certain outcomes; attempting, by sheer, dogged persistence to strong-arm the future into giving us what we want.

We tend to think that, because the heart is not linear, it must not be practical; because it is gentle, it must not be powerful. However, we must understand that, for all of its mystery and unpredictability, the heart loses absolutely nothing in the way of practicality and effectiveness. Far from being a frivolous or optional adornment to our lives, the feminine heart has tremendous power to manifest, effortlessly and in astonishing ways, all that we need in this physical world. However, working with the heart's infinite creativity demands a deep level of trust, devotion, and awareness.

Heart-Creation

There are certain ways of understanding the mechanism of heart creation that can help our linear, rational brains relax into trust.[18] As we will see, there is a dramatic difference in outcome when we create with the mind versus creating with the heart.[19]

Let us begin with the physical formation of these two organs, which offers a clue into the way they operate in the ethereal realms. The brain is split into two, polarized hemispheres. As a result, when we create with the mind, we cannot help but create a polarized reality. It is possible that what we conceive of with the mind will come to pass, but, as indicated by the physical construction of that organ, we can expect to be hit in some way by an equal-and-opposite force. The mind creates in order to get something it believes is lacking. This implies separation from what it wants, a gap which is filled with desire, a non-unity with that which it wants. Any gesture born from a sense of separation and lack cannot help but reinforce the illusion of separation and of lack.[20] Any choice made from desire will simply perpetuate and amplify desire instead of quenching or nourishing the need.

---

[18] The feminine power does, after all, operate according to logic, but it is a cosmic logic and adheres to laws that are generally far beyond the comprehension of our human minds.

[19] Thank you to Drunvalo Melchizedek who offered this initial framework for understanding the difference between mind and heart creation.

[20] People accustomed to creating with the mind often carry trauma and fear around taking action because, in their experience, any step toward their goals is accompanied inevitably by misfortune, calamity, abrupt tragedy, or anticlimax.

In contrast the heart is a unified organ connected deeply with the breath which is, of course, an ancient representation of spirit. The heart beats in rhythm, generating resonance and sending spirit, or prana, moving through every cell of the body. Each individual human heart is a perfect hologram of the universal heart, which creates and sustains all form. This means that within our own personal heart we hold the creation power of the universe. This is an immense realization- that we can literally create anything. Nothing is impossible when we engage the heart because within it resides the creative power of the universe.

The mechanism of heart-creation, a spiritual technology utilized by many ancient and advanced civilizations - and which is kept alive today through certain indigenous tribes across the globe- has been hidden from the larger collective for many eons. This is because it cannot be understood, or even accessed, until a certain level of consciousness has been reached.

Heart creation has built-in checks and balances. It is accessed only through the humble and sincere stance of authentic love. Therefore, it cannot be used to harm another; it cannot be used for personal gain at the expense of another; it cannot be manipulated, negotiated with, or forced into action. If we attempt to access the mechanism of heart-creation from self-interest, fear, or desire for retribution, it will simply not work. We can only access it from a place of genuine desire for the good of all beings.

This means that any creation or action that arises from the heart will automatically be aligned with the universal good. This understanding dissolves any guilt or fear attached to accepting the blessings that come to us. We can trust that when we dwell in the sacred space of our heart, all we create and all we receive is in harmony with the good of all.

Heart and Mind

    To enter the heart, we must let go of the whirring and clicking of our linear mind. We must draw our energy away from the ego and allow ourselves to be subsumed into trust of a larger power. It is at this threshold that humanity stands- the Great Change, the fraught cliff-edge of ego death. When our ego finally surrenders, when we finally open ourselves to the boundless experience of feeling everything within us, only then is the path to our hearts open, clear, and easily traversable. The mind relaxes into its natural state- a clear open space, its immense power laid down in service to love. It is then, when the masculine power of our mind falls to its knees, humbled and finally opened to the beauty and depth of love, do we finally merge with our sovereign nature- the part of us that is one with all. We become living testimonies of the power of the heart. Only those of us who have experienced this irreversible phenomenon can hope to lead others over the threshold and into the Eden on the other side.

    The description of a heart-centered way of being sounds much more complicated than the actual experience of it. When it finally happens, you move through the Earth in such a way that all of existence becomes aligned within you. Internal conflict subsides and your fears take on a far and distant quality, like a voice calling from somewhere far away. The world around you becomes suddenly simple, helpful, and poignant. You care for yourself more even as you find yourself needing less. You feel held within a larger force, which guides you simply, clearly, lovingly and, often, unpredictably. Your emotions arise, storms rage, but you live within the larger orb of space and sky; you become large enough to contain all of it. Sometimes you get caught in the drama of life, but these moments of arrest no longer define your existence. You simply notice you are caught and then untangle yourself from whatever briar or thorn captured you. In the untangling, you learn something about yourself, and you move forward.

The heart is not strategic. It can't be. Strategy implies a separation- a need to manipulate the outside world in order to "get" something that you don't have. This is not a concept that exists within the realm of the heart, as the heart *is* everything already. It contains all within it. According to the heart, there is absolutely no difference between having and being. The heart simply *is* all things. In this way, the heart always moves toward connection, honesty, openness, and transparency as, for the heart, there can be nothing whatsoever to hide. The heart is naturally intimate, revealing, and unselfconscious. You will know when something emanates from the heart because it empowers all of those around it. It speaks in ways that are transparent, truthful, and centered.

Because the heart is fearless, it is also disruptive. It loves all, attaches to nothing, and is unable to cater to the ego. It holds the innocence and purity of the divine, naturally illuminating all that is not in alignment with love. This illumination of truth is extremely challenging to those who live by mind-and-ego-centered systems. This is why, in the past, we have seen so many heart-centered figures martyred, brutalized, persecuted, and killed for expressing their deepest truth. The power of their love was a threat to any belief-system that was not itself founded on love.

Throughout all of the disruption, however, love is an inherently is a unifying force. Within you as an individual, the power of your love will necessarily sweep away all belief-systems that are not love. Eventually, your truth, and your refusal to betray yourself, will become a cohesive force even if, in the moment, it seems to create separation and conflict. Living according to the heart can be an intimidating prospect, but it is also a natural process and one that your heart and soul are ready for.

You are made of love. Your heart knows this. At the bottom of all you would call flaws, shadows, fears, and evil is simply, inevitably, the force of love. Your mind (and, of course, our collective mind), has spent many eons suppressing and denying this natural superpower, the result of this suppression being exhaustion, addiction, and what we would call "evil."

As heart power takes its place as the guiding light in our world, we do not create something new. Instead, we simply reveal and embrace the aspects of self that already exist. In this way, as we begin to harness the power of our heart, we come into a conscious, loving state of wholeness where all aspects of our being (even those parts we would have, at one point, sought to change, deny, or hide away) are reclaimed and re-membered as pure, unconditional love. In this place of openness and surrender we come to understand that everything is possible, the world is boundless, all is already within us, and miracles are truly available to us at all times. We release fear and become an embodiment of Eden, the natural, fertile ground of our highest expression. And, as Eden comes to rest in our consciousness, we watch in wonder as the secret garden- our inner Eden- manifests effortlessly in the world around us.

Receiving

Ultimately, Eden will be given unto us. It is not something we can conceptualize, theorize about, or understand. It is not something we create or force into being. It is, quite simply, something we receive. It is the final gift of our lives, bestowed after centuries of walking through darkness and suffering. Through our suffering we have been opened. And you must know: we *have* been opened. It is done. The darkness truly is lifting. The dawn is breaking. It is time now to receive all of the light, joy, and blessings that are positively bursting toward us.

Our final test, then, will be to allow this opening, and to receive. We are afraid, so afraid of receiving. In a world full of darkness we have all of us been wounded by receiving. We have received that which is toxic, cruel, unkind, manipulative. And even as the unkindness poured in, we were told to be grateful. We have been admonished to be grateful for that which was resentfully given. And so, we have shut ourselves off from receiving anything at all.

It is time to let that all fall away. Eden is not given resentfully or with condition. It is given as the rain is given. As the sun is given. As our bodies have been given. Eden arises from the sacred heart of the world, which is as unconditional as it is limitless, as loving as it is free. We are wounded no longer, and so, as we receive, gratitude arises as simply, as effortlessly as breath. It feels like joy. It feels like dancing in the rain. It feels like the spray of frost across a windowpane, gilded by the rising sun.

We have spent so many years tilting blindly at the windmills of our fears because we know that the moment we stop, we will open. The floodgates of our lives will part, and we will finally feel all that the world has to offer. And that opening terrifies us more than we can say.

Yet the truth is that we have nothing to fear in this world. The heart is yin, but it is not passive. It holds a vast intelligence that instantly recognizes what is and is not coming from a place of purity and love. It is a highly attuned instrument, able to see at once through the games and machinations of the ego. When confronted by that which is small, fearful, sharp, judgmental, or manipulative, it does not resist, yet it is not moved. The heart cannot identify with these things. It feels no need to challenge or resist them, nor does it hold these things as truth. In the light of love, these things dissolve, powerless. Therefore, the heart fears nothing. All that it connects with is love; all that is not love cannot survive its light.

The part of us that is afraid is the very part that will be washed away when the heart opens. That small part of us is fearful and so, we have shut down our hearts to soothe it. As a result, we have become dry and brittle inside, terrified of the anguish of being opened, terrified of all of the bad things that may take up residence if we swing wide the gates of our deepest, most tender sanctuary.

Yet, the heart is bigger than suffering, bigger than fear. What we experience as "receiving" is quite simply the heart welcoming another aspect of self. As you continue to welcome aspects of self, denying nothing, you become whole. You become free.

So, it is time to open. As you do, old, entangled thought forms will break apart, leaving your mind relaxed and ready to drink in the nectar of the divine mind. Finally, you will find the difference between exhaustion and peace, between resignation and surrender. You will see that stillness is not stagnation, and gentleness is not weak. Your heart is calling- its gates open wide before you. It is time to step over its threshold and come to rest, finally, in the boundless space that is your very own secret garden- the in-dwelling and eternal Eden.

Part II: Visualizations for Embodying the New Eden

Initiating Conscious Re-Birth

The image is the language of dreams and of life within.
The image is "sovereign life."
The image is the magic of space and the perfect instant- A moment outside of linear time that builds one luminous point after another- A time that is vertical in duration. The image is life which comes to help life, and is the movement of life, that starts life moving again.
… I propose to you to live some of those instants where the reversing of a desperate situation takes place before our eyes through an image:
"Close your eyes. Breathe out and imagine…"

-Colette Aboulker-Muscat
Mea Culpa: Tales of Resurrection

An Invitation to Enter

Welcome. You stand now at the threshold of your own luminous heart. The gates to Eden have been flung wide before you.

The portal opens in front of you, beckoning you with joy into unknown terrain. The doorway glimmers and breathes, expanding and contracting with the beat of your heart. It is your portal, your very own, alive, and pulsing with light.

This, you realize, is a familiar image, one that lives tucked away in the holy of holies, the most sacred realm of your being. It is your most closely-guarded secret. You recognize this portal, this doorway of light, as one you have seen many times before. And suddenly you remember. Again and again you have stood here at this moment of birth, but never before has the knowledge of it moved upward into your waking consciousness.

This is the moment for which you have yearned for so long without knowing it. It is the final answer to your seeking. After so many lifetimes of searching through the shifting sands of phenomena, you stand at last at the firm, unyielding threshold that will take you beyond your final longing. You have arrived once and for all at the conscious stepping through into oneness, the final exit from samsara. Just beyond this door of light is the place where you remember all, always and forever. Here, at last, is the place beyond forgetting.

Instinctively, you breathe in unison with the widening womb before you. With the next inspiration, your last breath, the final taking in of spirit, you step over the threshold and into the light.

Visualization for Sacred Protection

Prepare your space; find somewhere quiet and comfortable where you will not be disturbed. This is your time, just for you, to rest and connect with the boundless life of your inner world.

Sit or lie comfortably. Close your eyes and breathe deeply. Follow the silken stream of your breath as it flows into your lungs. Notice what emotions, thoughts, and reactions surface as you begin to focus on your breath.

Allow your eyes and the muscles around your eyes to relax. Allow your jaw and tongue to relax, releasing tension deep in your throat. Let your limbs become pleasantly heavy.

A shimmering, diamond-bright pyramid rises around and above you. It glints with gold and tourmaline, moonstone and amethyst. It holds you in an inviolable field of fierce protection. You suddenly know beyond doubt that you are safe and cared for, and all of your needs are met. Rest in this feeling for a moment, of being safe and cared for, of knowing that all of your needs are met. Snuggle in, like a child held in a mother's arms.

A golden vortex opens before you, rotating slowly. This is a divine portal, ready to remove anything you no longer want to carry. Anything you place into this vortex will disappear from your life forever.

Purse your lips and breathe out slowly, but with some force, as if blowing out a row of candles. You will take five deep breaths this way.

With the first exhale, watch the tension flowing out from all of your muscles. The tension leaves on your breath and is sent into the golden vortex, taken far, far away, never to return. Without thinking, without trying, simply notice what it looks like as it leaves you.

With your second exhale, watch the excess fire and sparks of your nervous system flowing out on your stream of breath. Without thinking, without trying, notice what it looks like as it leaves you. This energy streams directly into the vortex and is carried far, far away, never to return.

With your third exhale, watch as all density and stuckness lodged in all of your cells unlodges and flows out on the stream of your breath. Without thinking, without trying, notice what it looks like as it leaves you. This energy streams directly into the vortex and is carried far, far away, never to return.

With your fourth exhale, watch as all of the thoughts and stories of the outside world gather in one reservoir and then flow out on the stream of your breath. Without thinking, without trying, notice what it looks like as it leaves you. This energy streams directly into the vortex and is carried far, far away, never to return.

With your final cleansing exhale, let anything that is still left within you, anything you still want to let go of, come out on the stream of your breath. You do not have to know what it is; simply let it go. Without thinking, without trying, notice what it looks like as it leaves you. This energy streams directly into the vortex and is carried far, far away, never to return.

The golden vortex gently closes up, disappearing into a tiny pinprick of light. Then, all becomes dark and still.

Take a moment to rest in your body and notice the effect of this release. Feel the spaciousness of your body now that all of that extra energy and density has been siphoned away.

Let your breathing return to a rhythm that feels natural and unforced. The air around you has become golden and bright, flowing with light codes. As you breathe, the light enters your body effortlessly. Feel the light codes streaming in. The light flows into your skin, your organs, your bones, filling the spaces that have just opened in you, irradiating your whole body with a bright, golden, diamond light.

Feel your body opening like a flower in the sun as it becomes flooded with these new light codes.

An image floats into view. You see a tight, tangled mass of dark wires. What do they look like? How does it feel to behold them? Breathe out three times as you view the knotted and tangled wires. As you breathe, any rising emotions that you no longer want to hold are released, filtered out through the top of the diamond-bright pyramid that surrounds you.

(Pause for three breaths)

With your healing breath you blow on the tangled wires. Dust, dirt, crust, and density fall way from them and are filtered out through the top of the pyramid. The true nature of the wires is revealed- bright and golden and shining. You breathe on them again, and they become supple and alive. Slowly, as you watch, they begin to untangle, the tight knots loosening. You can see space now between the wires. They do this on their own. There is no need for you to do anything or force it to happen. Simply witness as it happens.

(Pause to witness)

You look at your hands and see that they are long-fingered and luminous. These are hands of light. These hands are healing hands, with the infinite potential to heal anything they touch.

With one long-fingered, luminous hand, you reach out to hold the wires. With one, brisk shake the wires completely untangle, and expand into a beautiful, golden web. You can see light pulsing through the web, clean and unobstructed. Watch for a moment as the web pulses and glimmers with life. Then the web expands even more and surrounds you. It forms an egg of light around you outlined with sacred geometric patterns.

You are now resting within powerful, protective, and alive energy field. Pause for a moment to see how this affects your body.

(Pause and witness)

Feel as the pulse of your body comes into harmony with the synapses of the golden web. Feel the thrum of energy flowing freely and unobstructed through your limbs, your spine, your brain. Feel light and energy rushing through your joints and ligaments, your tendons and nerves.

As you look up, you see that the space within the egg is inscribed with light codes. These codes are alive. They shimmer and dance, taking shape, dissolving, and taking shape again. As you watch, the light codes form a message for you. The message is delivered effortlessly into your consciousness. Even if you are not aware of it now, it will make itself known to you. You will not need to think about it or try to understand. Relax and breathe in the message from your higher self.

(Pause to receive the message)

Take a deep, cleansing breath and rest for a moment in your body and in your glimmering, pulsing, beautiful egg of light. Notice how it feels to be completely free and unobstructed.

(Pause and notice)

Gradually, keeping your eyes closed, become aware of your physical body. Bring movement into your fingers, your toes, your ankles, your shoulders. With eyes still closed, raise your right hand, and gently but firmly tap your sternum several times to imprint this feeling of into your body. Now that you have felt it, you can return to this feeling any time. It lives in your body now and cannot be removed.

Still letting yourself feel the feelings of being completely unobstructed, let your eyes open. Remain this way for a few moments as you take in your surroundings, still letting your body rest in its new knowledge.

And gradually, when you're ready, move back into your waking life.

Before you engage in any practical tasks, take time to journal, write, or create a voice recording to reflect on what you experienced. Note how you feel, and what has changed for you. This act of reflection will even more firmly imprint the experience into your body.

Chapter 3: Purpose

Teachings of Purpose

"What is your purpose?"

It is a question that swirls through our busy world. When you are tuned in, any answer you try to give becomes caught in your throat. Your purpose is a nameless thing. It is nothing more and nothing less than the living prayer of your life, the wholeness of your being consecrated in service to that which you know to be true. It cannot be spoken of, only lived.

Your purpose reveals itself like a flower, petal by petal, choice by choice. It is the one thing more compelling than your fears. It is the irresistible thread of wonder that leads you in and out, in and out again from darkness. It speaks to you through desire, through curiosity, through laughter, through love. It speaks to you through rage and those moments when you feel helpless. It dawns slowly, and when it arrives, it seems as though it has always been.

Your purpose will lead you even as it abides within you. It is not separate from you, it *is* you.

What is your wisdom?

What is your suffering?

What is the one thing that only you know?

Purpose is your innermost secret, the thing you have hidden even from yourself, that you spend a lifetime seeking.

--

Purpose will not be found "out there." How often do you charge into the world, forcibly setting it to rights, demanding that it bow to your preferences, your ideas, your beliefs of what it "should" be?

You tilt at windmills and get thrown back, bruised, while the windmill stands, unaffected, dancing its stately dance. You knock down the straw men of your fears in the name of justice. You do this and your fears find you again in another disguise. All around you see "that which is wrong," and you set out to make it right. The act of "making it right" becomes your rallying cry. This must be it! You exclaim. My purpose! And you drain your life force in postures of resistance.

When you finally dive below the fears and the righteousness, you find the root of this impulse of resistance. It is love. Only love. You see suffering- your own and that of others- and in the moment it is easier to fight than to feel. You launch a crusade to rid the world of suffering. The crusade becomes your purpose. But it does not work. Again and again, the world throws you back on yourself, and the suffering marches on. It is so easy, then, to become overwhelmed, to give up, to check out from the world and your deep, inviolable caring of it. You cannot go on and you cannot stop. In a world such as this, it is negligent to sit still. You must *do* something! Right?

Then, perhaps, one day, you do the unthinkable. You become still. As you become still, the chaos within reveals itself, and you let it. You let it. Eventually, it calms itself, and the waters of your being become clear.

You find something else, something astonishing. You find that, as you change, the world does also. As you become quiet, so too does the world. As you become gentle, so too do those around you. As you love, so too does the world love you. After years of trying so hard and not making the slightest dent in the suffering of the world, it was this simple inward turning that has done it. You didn't conquer fear by arming yourself against it. You conquered it by becoming it; by dissolving into it, by discovering that it never was and never will be.

As you do this, so too does all of humanity.

-

You understand that your fears will never lead you where you want to go. What then, will? Perhaps your longing, perhaps your desires, perhaps your wonder, perhaps your joy. You follow these things, sometimes holding them blindly, as though gripping a rope in a blizzard. A slender thing, to hold your life in this way. But you have the rope. So many do not even have that.

You begin to operate by a different set of rules, the ones that uphold your worthiness and dignity. It is a breathtaking moment of freedom, to lift up and out of the rules of the world, to discover there is a whole other plane of existence that does not care a bit for the rules that held you like chains.

You begin to command kindness, abundance, generosity, prosperity, fulfillment, simplicity, all without the help of the rules that had bound you for so long.

Nothing binds you now. In this new place everything is possible, and nothing is necessary. The freedom is overwhelming at times. You spin sometimes, looking for someone, something to guide you. You no longer fit into your old skin, but what of the new skin? Some days you aren't quite sure how to wear it.

When you merge with your heart, you no longer seek guidance, not even from God. When this happens, your purpose manifests in flesh and blood and bone.

Visualization for Embodying Purpose

Prepare your space; find somewhere quiet and comfortable where you will not be disturbed. This is your time, just for you, to rest and connect with the boundless life of your inner world.

Sit or lie comfortably. Close your eyes and breathe deeply. Follow the smooth stream of your breath as it flows into your lungs. Notice what emotions, thoughts, and reactions surface as you begin to focus on your breath. Let these float through you and fall away, like a leaf on the breeze.

Allow your eyes, and the muscles around your eyes to relax. Allow your jaw and tongue to relax. Let your limbs become pleasantly heavy.

A shimmering, diamond-bright pyramid rises around and above you. It glints with gold and tourmaline, moonstone, amethyst, sapphire, and pearl. It holds you in an inviolable field of fierce protection. You are safe and cared for, and all of your needs are met. Rest in this feeling for a moment, of being safe and cared for, of knowing that all of your needs are met. Snuggle in, like a child held in the arms of a loving mother.

A golden vortex opens before you, rotating slowly. It is a divine portal, ready to remove anything you no longer want to carry. Anything you place into this vortex will disappear from your life forever.

Purse your lips and breathe out slowly, but with some force, as if blowing out a row of candles. You will take five deep breaths this way.

With the first exhale, watch the tension flowing out from all of your muscles. It leaves on the breath and is sent into the golden vortex, taken far, far away, never to return. Without thinking, without trying, simply notice what it looks like as it leaves you.

With your second exhale, watch the excess fire and sparks of your nervous system flowing out on your stream of breath. Without thinking, without trying, notice what it looks like as it leaves you. This energy streams directly into the vortex and is carried far, far away, never to return.

With your third exhale, watch as all density and stuckness lodged in all of your cells unlodges and flows out on the stream of your breath. Without thinking, without trying, notice what it looks like as it leaves you. This energy streams directly into the vortex and is carried far, far away, never to return.

With your fourth exhale, watch as all of the thoughts and stories of the outside world gather in one reservoir and then flow out on the stream of your breath. Without thinking, without trying, notice what it looks like as it leaves you. This energy streams directly into the vortex and is carried far, far away, never to return.

With your final breath, let anything that is still left within you, anything you still want to let go of, come out on the stream of your breath. You do not have to know what it is; simply let it go. Without thinking, without trying, notice what it looks like as it leaves you. This energy streams directly into the vortex and is carried far, far away, never to return.

The vortex gently closes up, disappearing into a tiny pinprick of light. Then, all becomes dark and still.

Take a moment to rest in your body and notice the effect of this release.

(Pause and notice)

All around you is a tranquil, welcoming darkness. You are aware that you do not have a body or form. You exist only as pure consciousness. It is peaceful here, quiet and restful. It is such a nice place to be, this darkness. Rest here for a moment in pure awareness.

(Pause and rest)

From the center of the darkness, you witness a single, brilliant shaft of pure, white light, whiter than white. It emanates from the darkness. You understand that what you are seeing is the birth of your soul. You have come back to this moment before time in order to witness it.

The shaft of light is made of sound, of a very specific frequency. Allow this sound, now, to emanate from your own throat. Without thinking, without trying, without effort, just let it happen.

(Pause to tone, out loud, the frequency that brought your soul into being)

This sound is *your* sound. It is the original frequency of your soul. You understand you can heal yourself with this sound. You understand you can create anything with this sound.

The shaft of light continues to emanate from the center of the darkness. You move toward the light with your consciousness and then enter into it fully.

As your consciousness meets the light of your soul, let yourself become an explosion of light. You *are* this light, this explosion. As the pure light of your soul meets your consciousness, it splinters into a thousand colors, like when sunlight meets a crystal prism. You see the beauty and complexity of your soul as it shatters into shafts of the most beautiful, jewel-bright colors- aquamarine, carnelian, emerald, sapphire, ruby, violet and topaz, pearl and rose, and so many colors you have never seen before. Your consciousness, the place where you entered the shaft of light, remains in place. It enables the original pure light of your soul to burst completely into all of the colors of the universe, shining out into eternity. Rest for a moment and witness this sight.

(Pause and behold)

You become aware that each color of your soul contains its own unique quality and travels on its own unique journey. Each of these colors of your soul lives through its own odyssey, experiencing a full arc of lifetimes and experiences.

Far, far in the distance you sense that there is a place where all of these colors merge together again. At that point of merging, the colors have become pregnant and heavy, encoded with lifetimes of wisdom.

Still existing as free and formless consciousness, you move forward to that point of merging, far in the distance. As you go, you play with the colors running beneath you. You dip in and out of them as a dragonfly alights on water. Move toward any color, any frequency that draws you, and stay as long as you wish. As you experience the different frequencies of your soul, notice what images, sensations, messages, or sounds arise. This is a time of lightness and exploration, for you to become acquainted with parts of the many, many incarnations your soul has traveled through.

(Long pause for exploration, play, and witnessing)

You gradually become aware that you are hovering above an emerald-green meadow, strewn with wildflowers. This is the sanctuary of your heart, the place within you that is unchanging and always peaceful. This is the point of stillness, the aspect of you that retains the memory of your origin. This heart-sanctuary abides, whole, untouched, and accessible, within each of your soul's incarnations. It holds all of the records of your existence. It is a wormhole to re-membering, the direct point of access to the pure light of your original soul.

    Simply abide here. Without thinking, without trying, notice if any messages arise.

(Pause to witness and listen)

    It is time now to call back the splintered lights of your soul, the jewel-bright frequencies that traveled for so long and so far, and that gathered so much wisdom. It is time now for your final re-membering.

    From the depths of you, allow the tone, the sound that called your soul into being, to sing out once again. Let the primordial vibration rise from the depths of your heart. This is the frequency of purity and wholeness that called the light of your soul forward from the welcoming darkness. Let it emanate now from your chest, shaped by your throat and given life through your sacred breath.

(Pause to tone for as long as feels good).

    Immediately the air begins to shimmer and dance around you. All of the colors of your soul have been called back to you by the sound of your voice. They materialize and begin to swirl in a joyful whirlwind around where you hover, a formless center-point of consciousness, a single origin of sound and vibration and will. Let yourself be swept up in this whirlwind of color. Notice that each color is comprised of light codes that swirl together, forming sacred geometric shapes. These rays of soul light are heavy and pregnant with the wisdom gathered over their long journeys through the universe.

    The light rays swirl and dance, coming together around you. As the colors come together, they merge with your formless will and begin to take shape. This is the shape of your highest divine self. You understand that your current incarnation is the one that is ready to hold, in wholeness, the many, many light codes, the deep wisdom, and the divine mastery of your soul. Watch as the colors come together. What form do they create? Watch, witness, feel, and allow.

(Long pause to witness)

This form is you- your higher self. This is your complete rainbow body, the whole of you gathered together into one full expression, one potent incarnation pregnant and quivering with fertility. There is something this form was designed to be. There is something that this form was designed to create in this lifetime. This being, this creation, reclaims and utilizes *all* of your wisdom, experience, and understandings. With this creation, there is nothing left over, nothing left behind. All that is you is needed to bring this being, this creation, to life. What is that state of being? What is that creation? Without thinking, without trying, listen for the answer. When the answer comes, you will know. It will be simple and obvious, and it will kindle a fire of joy in your heart.

(Long pause to listen)

Take a deep, cleansing breath and rest for a moment in your rainbow body of light. Notice how it feels to have all parts of you gathered together in the form of your highest self. Notice how it feels to be whole again.

Gradually, keeping your eyes closed, become aware of your physical body. With eyes still closed, raise your right hand, and gently but firmly tap your sternum several times to imprint the message of your deepest purpose into your body. Now that you have felt it, it is within your waking consciousness. It lives in your body now and cannot be removed or taken away from you.

Still letting yourself feel the feelings of wholeness and purpose, let your eyes open. Remain this way for a few moments as you take in your surroundings, still letting your body rest in its new knowledge.

And gradually, when you're ready, move back into your waking life.

Before you engage in any practical tasks, take time to journal, write, or create a voice recording to reflect on what you experienced. Note how you feel, and what has changed for you. This act of reflection will even more firmly imprint the experience into your body.

Chapter 4: Integrity

Teachings of Integrity

Integrity is so simple that many forego it, seeking answers more complex. But there is no mystery to it. It is a place of clarity where yes means yes, and no means no. With integrity you do not play games, you do not bargain, you do not plead, apologize, nor explain. You do not live in falsehood, not in word nor in deed. With integrity, there is nothing to explain, nothing to defend, nothing to hide. You live transparently and cease to worry about who will, or will not, notice.

If purpose is the path to flourishing, integrity is the compass. It is a living needle pointing always True North. It is the word you speak, the choice you make, that resonates with your soul.

We saw the Earth and God in their cosmic dance. We know that we cannot make a mistake, that all decisions lead, eventually, to our flourishing. Yet, we can choose direct and loving paths to our fulfillment, paths of release that navigate suffering with grace and trust. This is the path of your truth. Your truth is not what you have heard, not what you think. It is the pulse of your blood, the drumbeat of your heart, the unbidden rising of words in your throat. Anything demanding untruth is not worth what it promises. Untruth is an invitation to suffering.

With integrity your divine will makes itself known, unmistakable and undeniable as breath. You see at once that no person, no system, no thought, no human law has power over you.

In this place there is no room for compromise. There is no such thing as a "small" betrayal. You listen for the drop in your chest, the failing of strength, when considering the choices before you. What is the voice of truth? Sometimes it calls strident from the center of your heart; sometimes it nudges you gently, a small push in a certain direction.

When we say someone has "integrity," we often mean that they do what they say they will do. But it is time that we demand more of ourselves. We must dig now into the very heart of our purpose. We must decide what truly matters to us. When we do as we say, we are "reliable." But you may agree to that which is draining, uninspiring, wrong. You may agree to something that goes against the grain of your soul. To follow through on such a thing brings harm into the world. To break this agreement and, standing upright, accept the consequences, that is integrity.

Eventually you become sensitive as the dowsing rod, crossing the heart at boundaries of truth. You consider completely the value of your word, your energy, your precious presence, and you give it only where it flows naturally, where it leaps with joy. To all else, you say "no." You listen for the "no" within you, you locate it within a single cell of your body, and then your whole being becomes a "no." When presented with opportunities, you feel the slight drag of reluctance, and, though your mind may clamor, may list all of the advantages, you feel only that drag, that subtle heaviness. It arises, not from fear, not from a lack of will, but from an intelligence beyond what you can understand. You feel the drag, and you understand it must be a "no." Eventually, the wisdom of that "no" is revealed to you. Soon, there is no need to backtrack and make amends, because you have learned to listen to the voice of your omniscient heart: when it says yes, and when it says no.

Some days you walk through life as though surrounded by a cloud of flies, buzzing, biting, challenging your every thought, every decision. There is a cacophony of voices within that argue over the smallest movement of your finger, your every breath. When you turn toward these voices, they exhaust you. You try to placate, explain, justify, but despite your efforts, they clamor on. Integrity is the force that clears away these voices, these biting flies. Integrity is the unmistakable command of authority, dignity, and will. It reminds you that the flies, the voices, are habit rather than truth. With integrity you become certain in your movements. You cease to question.

The lightning rod channels the pulse of the sky. It seems impossibly thin to conduct such force. Its strength comes, not from its size, but from its alignment. But it *must* be aligned or it will shatter upon contact. You have been created to command, to channel, to direct impossibly large forces. Integrity is the power of your alignment, the orientation toward that which is always true. As you stand in perfect alignment, you conduct the light of the heavens.

Integrity will not ensure an outcome. It does not bargain, it does not amass credit, and it does not have memory. It can be accessed only now; it concerns only what is immediately in front of you. This choice may be different tomorrow, but integrity does not think about tomorrow. Tomorrow is only a figment, and integrity is concerned only with what is real, what is now.

Integrity will move through you like the wind in autumn. You will watch the withered parts of you detach and fall like rain to the Earth. Integrity waits only for your surrender. With it, you divest yourself of weight, of density, of darkness, and of uncertainty, of that which has died. Soon, all that's left is the thin needle of the compass and the next, perfect step to which it points.

It sounds like a lofty thing, integrity, but indeed it is so very ordinary. It scorns nothing. It is present in all that your hands do throughout the day. Notice the humble things your hands do each day- holding a book, gripping a pen, buttoning your shirt, holding a loved one. Integrity is present wherever you are honest, and your hands are always honest.

Integrity recognizes itself in another. You may respect an angry man more than a quiet one. The angry one may be honest while the quiet one holds back truth. You will sense this, and like the compass needle, you will point toward what is true, regardless of appearances.

In integrity, you return again and again to the depths of you, that still and quiet space abiding beneath thought, beneath words, beneath reason. It resides as a deep well of your being. With it, you draw each choice, each word like a brimming bucket from that well. You drink of its truth, and you willingly to behold that which is brought up from the depths.

How can *you*, a being so complex, ever come into alignment? Won't there always be war? Conflict? Doubt? No. But only integrity can do this. It is the ringing bell that brings all into harmony. It rises on the upward turn of your being, transcending the clamor and cacophony, the doubt and the questions. It is the voice of your heart, the one that needs no explanation, whispering you always into completion.

Visualization for Embodying Integrity

Prepare your space; find somewhere quiet and comfortable where you will not be disturbed. This is your time, just for you, to rest and connect

Sit or lie comfortably. Close your eyes and breathe deeply. Follow the silken stream of your breath as it flows into your lungs. Notice what emotions, thoughts, and reactions surface as you begin to focus on your breath. Let them drift away, light and insubstantial, like clouds.

Allow your eyes and the muscles around your eyes to relax. Allow your jaw and tongue to relax. Feel your tongue relaxing deep in your throat. Let your limbs become pleasantly heavy. Feel your muscles unwind, starting at your toes, your ankles, up your calves and hamstrings, tension is unraveling. Up your hips and lower back, waves of soft light washing constriction and worry from the muscles around your spine, your jaw, your face, your forehead, your eyes, your crown. A wave of relaxation cascades down your shoulders, your arms, flowing out your fingertips. Feel your body tingling and letting go.

Watch as a shimmering diamond-bright pyramid rises around and above you. It glints with gold and tourmaline, moonstone and amethyst, sapphire and ruby and emerald. It holds you in an inviolable field of calm and protection. You are safe and cared for, and all of your needs are met. Rest in this feeling for a moment, of being safe and cared for, of knowing that all of your needs are and always will be met. Snuggle into this feeling like a child held in the arms of a loving mother.

A golden vortex opens before you, rotating slowly. It is a divine portal, ready to remove anything you no longer want to carry. Anything you place into this vortex will be released from your life forever.

Purse your lips and breathe out slowly, but with some force, as if blowing out a row of candles. You will take five deep breaths this way.

With the first exhale, watch any remaining tension flowing out from all of your muscles. It leaves on the breath and is sent into the golden vortex, taken far, far away, never to return. Without thinking, without trying, simply notice what it looks like as it leaves you. Notice any sensations, memories, or thoughts that surface as you let it go.

With your second exhale, watch the excess fire and sparks of your nervous system flowing out on your stream of breath. Without thinking, without trying, notice what it looks like as it leaves you. This sparking energy streams directly into the vortex and is carried far, far away, never to return.

With your third exhale, watch as all density and stuckness lodged in all of your cells unlodges and flows out on the stream of your breath. Without thinking, without trying, notice what it looks like as it leaves you. This energy streams directly into the vortex and is carried far, far away, never to return.

With your fourth exhale, watch as all of the thoughts and stories of the outside world gather in one reservoir and then flow out on the stream of your breath. Without thinking, without trying, notice what it looks like as it leaves you. This energy streams directly into the vortex and is carried far, far away, never to return.

With your final breath, let anything that is still left within you, anything you still want to let go of, come out on the stream of your breath. You do not have to know what it is; simply let it go. Without thinking, without trying, notice what it looks like as it leaves you. This energy streams directly into the vortex and is carried far, far away, never to return.

The vortex gently closes up, disappearing into a tiny pinprick of light. Then, all becomes dark and still.

Take a moment to rest in your body and notice the effect of this release. Feel the spaciousness of your body now that all of that extra energy and density has been siphoned away.

(pause to feel)

You find yourself in a thick fog. You cannot see through the fog, not even when you lift a hand in front of your eyes. You are not frightened, as you know you are safe and protected. You stand and breathe slowly. Each of your exhales clears some of the fog away, until gradually your surroundings begin to reveal themselves.

Pause and breathe three deep breaths, watching the fog slowly disappear.

(pause to breathe and watch)

As you finish your third exhale, you notice you are standing in a dark, dense, forest, closely surrounded by brambles and thickets. You cannot walk in any direction; the forest is too dark and closed in around you. Dark green trees, so dark as to be almost black, arch above you blocking out the sky. What does it feel like to be standing here?

You reach into your pocket and feel a cool, metal disc as large as the palm of your hand. You pull it out of your pocket and look down at it.

In your hand is a shining compass. It is bright gold, shining with its own light. The bright light of the compass illuminates your face and the surroundings, like a small star in your hand.

As you look at the compass, you notice the needle on the face begin to spin. It spins until it becomes a blur, then it slows down, slows, and slows and finally stops, pointing in one direction.

You turn and face the direction in which it points.

As you look up, a shining path forms through the dark thicket. The path forms effortlessly, easily dissolving the dark brambles and thorned bushes. It is carpeted with bright, golden leaves, and above the path you can see the sky, delicate blue as a robin's egg.

As you stand there and behold the path, you sense an animal standing at your left. It has joined you to offer its support and love. Glance over. What or whom do you see standing next to you? Don't think, analyze, or question. Just take the first image that arises. The animal may have a message for you. Listen.

(pause to listen)

Putting the compass back in your pocket, you look up. Immediately in front of you is an archway of light. It marks the entrance to the golden path that sparkles with sunshine, glinting and winking with diamond light. You take a deep breath and step through the archway and onto the path, first one foot and then the next. You understand that, on some level of your being, you have just made an important decision.

The thicket is now behind you, barely visible through the archway. You are surrounded by space and air, stretches of sunlit meadow rolling in soft, undulating hills. It is sprinkled with violets and cornflowers, aster and yellow bells and starflower. Their fragrance, mingling with sunwarmed grass, wafts on the light breeze. Take a moment to look around.

(short pause)

Now look back to the path unfolding ahead of you. How does your body feel, standing on this path?

You step forward again and feel as though you have walked into a large, sticky spider web. You do not panic, because you know you are safe and held. Instead, you stand still and, with your next breath, you summon a soft, violet flame to rise from beneath your feet. You close your eyes and feel the violet flame rising from the path. It burns up the spiderweb but cannot burn you because it is your creation. The flames rise around you, pleasantly warm and tingling. You breathe out, and the spiderweb is gone. The flames recede. You take another, bolder step on your path. You understand that, whatever arises on your path, it cannot hurt you. You have everything you need to safely, effortlessly, and creatively clear anything that may materialize in front of you.

You walk along peacefully, taking deep breaths of the fresh air.

You reach back into your pocket and find a folded scrap of paper. You pull it out and open it. Something is written on the paper, and you recognize your own handwriting. It is a question. This question has been living for some time within you, but you have not yet given it voice. Here, in this place where you are safe and unafraid you can read the question clearly. What is the question that is written on this paper?

(pause to read the question)

You take the compass back out of your pocket. It sits cool and comforting in your hand. You ask it the question.

The needle on the compass spins into a blur. The path and meadow fade away as the compass spins. Then it slows, slows, and finally stops. You turn in the direction that the needle is pointing in. You look up. What do you see?

Without thinking, analyzing, or judging, take a few minutes to rest in this space, where the compass brought you. There is no need to try or to do anything. Simply breathe and open yourself to receive. You may see beings or colors. You may smell fragrances or hear music or tones. You may feel the urge to speak out loud. You may receive messages, or you may see or feel nothing at all. Trust that what you need is being transmitted to you.

(long pause)

Gradually, keeping your eyes closed, become aware of your physical body. Bring movement into your fingers, your toes, your ankles, your shoulders. With eyes still closed, raise your right hand, and gently but firmly tap your sternum several times to imprint the messages you received into your body.

Still letting yourself feel the truth of the messages you received, consciously or unconsciously, let your eyes open. Remain this way for a few moments as you take in your surroundings, still letting your body rest in its truth.

And gradually, when you're ready, move back into your waking life.

Before you engage in any practical tasks, take time to journal, write, or create a voice recording to reflect on what you experienced. Note how you feel, and what has changed for you. This act of reflection will even more firmly imprint the experience into your body.

Chapter 5: Emptiness

Teachings of Emptiness

You stand in the empty hall of your home. The air is ringing with the final slam of the door. The ego has departed at last, taking with it its piles of baggage, its heavy, dragging memories, its deafening clamor of discordant voices.

You have feared this moment as much as you have longed for it. What will this house be without the distractions, the drama, the addictions, the endless *doing* that has for so long kept you from yourself? Who will you be when you are no longer needed to hold together the world?

But it was time. To the ego, to your fears, doubts, and anxieties, to your criticisms and judgements, to your guilt and resentment, hatred and blame, to your insecurities and the voices that held you captive, to the clenched fists and tension, you bade "leave," and you stood watching as it all went. It had no choice but to respond to your command. In that moment, as you stood finally in the empty, echoing hall, you understood that you have always been the master here. All else was an illusion.

You stand now in the soft, vibrating stillness of a vast and empty house. Your house. Your very own.

You walk through quiet rooms seeing them as never before. In the liquid light of the setting sun, the rooms, *your* rooms, reveal themselves in new glory. Rich tapestries catch the light, unfurling and glowing in the brilliant sunset. You had never seen these before. You wander through the rooms, picking up trinkets that reveal themselves to be jewels, rare and precious, finely wrought, and priceless. Yours. All yours. You never knew.

All this time you thought you had been a prisoner with no right to these treasures. But you know now it had been yours all along, simply waiting for you to claim them.

The windows of your eyes become fathomless and clear. Stillness descends on your heart like a dove settling into its nest. You feel the weight and the warmth of the bird, the rightness of it, this final coming to rest. Gentle, tender as breath.

You have become the clarity of sky, free as unbound air. All that is heavy and loud, all that is bracing and constricted, all that is hard and sharp and heavy, all effort, striving, and need has been released. It fades even now as a dream upon awakening. You can barely remember the voices that had held you in their thrall. You would not recognize them again. You let them fade as your reality becomes, once and for all, this golden stillness, the breath of peace, this emptiness filled with light.

Visualization for Embodying Emptiness

Prepare your space; find somewhere quiet and comfortable where you will not be disturbed. This is your time, just for you, to rest and connect

Sit or lie comfortably. Close your eyes and breathe deeply. Follow the silken stream of your breath as it flows into your lungs. The air around you is infused with light. As you bring it into your lungs, it disperses through your body. The light you breathe is intelligent; it effortlessly delivers healing and nourishment to each of the different parts of your body, giving every cell exactly what it needs. Notice how your lungs become empty as you exhale. Notice a feeling of relaxation and wellbeing as you become effortlessly emptied and then filled again.

Allow your eyes to relax. Feel the muscles around your eyes relaxing and letting go. Allow your jaw and tongue to relax. Let your limbs become pleasantly heavy. A pleasant, warm energy begins to flow up your body, emanating from the Earth below. As it moves through you, it feels as though each part of your body expands beyond its physical dimensions. This energy washes into your feet, and your toes uncurl and expand. The muscles of your calves expand, your knees feel light and spacious. The energy washes up your thighs, your hips and lower back, waves of soft light washing tension and worry from the muscles around your spine, your jaw, your face, your forehead, your eyes, your crown. A wave of relaxation cascades down your shoulders, your arms, flowing out your fingertips. Feel your body as it takes on new dimensions.

A shimmering, diamond-bright pyramid rises around and above you. It glints with gold and tourmaline, moonstone, sapphire, violet, ruby and amethyst. It holds you in an inviolable field of calm protection. All density that you release from your body, your mind, your emotional body, and your spirit will be safely taken up and removed through the point of the pyramid. You are safe and cared for, and all of your needs are met. Rest in this feeling for a moment, of being safe and cared for, of knowing that all of your needs are, and always will be, met.

(Pause)

A golden vortex opens before you, rotating slowly, rising through the top of the pyramid. It is a divine portal, ready to remove anything you no longer want to carry. Anything you place into this vortex will be released from your life.

Purse your lips and breathe out slowly, but with some force, as if blowing out a row of candles. You will take five deep breaths this way.

With the first exhale, watch any remaining tension flowing out from all of your muscles. The tension leaves on the breath and is sent into the golden vortex, taken far, far away, never to return. Without thinking, without trying, simply notice what it looks like as it leaves you. Notice any sensations, memories, or thoughts that surface as you let it go.

With your second exhale, watch the excess fire and sparks of your nervous system flowing out on your stream of breath. Without thinking, without trying, notice what it looks like as it leaves you. This sparking energy streams directly into the vortex and is carried far, far away, never to return.

With your third exhale, watch as all density and stuckness lodged in all of your cells unlodges and flows out on the stream of your breath. Without thinking, without trying, notice what it looks like as it leaves you. This energy streams directly into the vortex and is carried far, far away, never to return.

With your fourth exhale, watch as all of the thoughts and stories of the outside world gather in one reservoir and then flow out on the stream of your breath. Without thinking, without trying, notice what it looks like as it leaves you. This energy streams directly into the vortex and is carried far, far away, never to return.

With your final breath, let anything that is still left within you, anything you still want to let go of, come out on the stream of your breath. You do not have to know what it is; simply let it go. Without thinking, without trying, notice what it looks like as it leaves you. This energy streams directly into the vortex and is carried far, far away, never to return.

The vortex gently closes up, disappearing into a tiny pinprick of light. Then, all becomes dark and still.

Take a moment to rest in your body and notice the effect of this release. Feel the shape and dimensions of your body.

(Pause and notice)

Bring your awareness to the place in your body where your consciousness resides. For most, it feels as though it rests just behind the eyes. Take a moment and gently place your awareness on the place where you find your consciousness is living. See your consciousness pulsing like a ball of golden light.

With delight and a sense of adventure, you discover that your consciousness can move locations. It can bring you anywhere you wish to go, showing you anything you wish to see, and communicating anything you would like to know. Let yourself revel in the feeling of freedom that arises as you consider the new world of possibilities opening to you.

(Pause)

Slowly, allow your consciousness to move backwards from behind your eyes. It travels slowly, a golden ball of light, and comes softly to rest in the very middle of your brain. Breathe light into this space, so that it expands, becoming brighter and brighter. How does it feel to experience the world from here? What can you see from this new vantage point? Allow sensations to arise as you breathe. You may experience visions, sensations, feelings, or memories arising as you rest here. What can you see? You do not have to try, or think, or do anything at all. Simply rest and allow and notice.

(Pause and witness)

You now bring your awareness into the golden ball of light. Step into it, so that your witnessing awareness and your experiencing consciousness are merged. Rest here for a moment as these two parts- the witnesser and the experiencer- integrate.

Slowly, encased in the golden ball of light, you begin to descend downward. Travel down your throat, past your sternum, and come to rest just behind your heart. Stand for a moment looking up at the temple of your heart. What do you see?

(Pause)

You notice a door in front of you and understand that it leads directly into your heart's temple. Take a moment to look at this door, taking in every detail of it. You step up to the door, and it opens. As the door opens it draws you effortlessly inward into the sacred space of your heart.

Allow the light of your awareness to illuminate your surroundings. Breathe deeply and look around. What does it look like here? What does it feel like to be here? Know that each time you return it may look and feel different.

Gradually, let all that you see fade away. Now there is nothing but a vast emptiness. All around is stillness and quiet. Everything heavy has dropped away, and nothing remains. There is nothing here.

There is no need to think or to do. Allow yourself to rest here, in the welcoming, dark stillness.

(Pause and rest)

Gradually, a form begins to take shape in the darkness. Here in the dark, still emptiness there is one thing resolving into form. It is your heart's deepest longing. Watch as it takes shape. This longing is your birthright. It is the origin your will. It is the shape of your destiny. Trust in this longing. What is it? Allow it to take shape. Touch that longing. Be with it. Be with all that it holds and all that arises in you as you behold it.

(Pause)

Allow the longing to dissolve into a wash of hope and energy. Feel yourself infused with vibrating energy. You understand that you are in the quickening, quivering, fertile space of the heart. You are absolutely free. You can create anything from here. You know that anything you create from this dark, vibrating space of your heart will carry the resonance of pure love. You feel a wash of joy and anticipation as you consider what you will bring forth into the world. Take a moment to play, as a child, in the sacred space of your heart. Know that anything is possible. Absolutely nothing is impossible to the divine mind.

Allow yourself to sit like a curious and watchful child in the womb of your heart. You may see images rise, unbidden, from the darkness. What do you see?

You may choose to create your own images. What do you create?

You may feel tones or vibrations rising in your chest. Give them voice, out loud if possible. These are your frequencies of creation.

Take time to rest, play, and be at peace here in the limitless space of creation.

(Pause)

Take one last look around and gradually, keeping your eyes closed, become aware of your physical body. Let your consciousness come to rest again behind your eyes. Bring movement into your fingers, your toes, your ankles, your shoulders. With eyes still closed, hold the new knowings, creations, possibilities, and the vibrations that you just experienced in your right hand. Raise your right hand, full of possibility, and firmly tap your sternum several times. This to imprint the possibilities your body. Know that all that you create from the space of your heart is possible. Know that your heart's longing is to be trusted absolutely and without doubt.

Still resting in emptiness, let your eyes open. Remain this way for a few moments as you take in your surroundings.

And gradually, when you're ready, move back into your waking life.

Before you engage in any practical tasks, take time to journal, write, or create a voice recording to reflect on what you experienced. Note how you feel, and what has changed for you. This act of reflection will even more firmly imprint the experience into your body.

Chapter 6: Presence

Teachings of Presence

Water is the teaching of presence. To be at once still and flowing, to be a clear reflection of all that looks upon it and yet utterly, wholly itself, such is presence.

Whisper to water and watch its very molecules form temples to your words. Whisper love to water, and drink in love. Whisper your hopes and dreams and the water, with the infinite wisdom of the universe, forms your answer. And as you drink, you bring that answer into your body.

Water is the crash of rapids and the gentle fall of rain. It is the mist of clouds, refracting the true nature of light. It is the pure whiteness of snow, the flakes crafted, one by one, by the hand of a master. It is the delicate feathers of frost on the window in the morning, painted in light, glittering frozen filigree, a gift from the hand of our maker, precious as diamonds, fleeting as breath.

Water is the emotional body of the Earth, the sensitive communication of realms unable to be accessed by the sharp, probing spear of the mind. Plunge a spear into water and it emerges again, dripping, frustrated. The water has affected the spear, but the spear has not affected the water. Its depths remain unplumbed, unknown. The mind cannot fathom the emotions, cannot reveal their secrets. Presence is not of the mind. It is the riverbed; it is the ground beneath the ocean. It is the holding of emotions, the merging with them to know their shape, their form, their wisdom.

The body itself is water. It is yin, receptive. The molecules of the body are mutable. They believe every word you say. They form temples to your words. The frequency of your words, rippling from the center of your throat, change the nature of your body, change the shape of your cells, the atoms that are you.

What is water? It is a lake. It is snow. It is the ocean. It is the rain. It is at once the charging rapids and the still pond. It is the avalanche. It is melted crystal. It is the glittering teeth of icicles.

What is water? How can it be all of these things? Your mind wants to know, but it can only recite facts. You cannot use the spear of your mind to know water. You cannot use the mind to know the body, or your life. You must become it.

Presence is the teaching of water. In presence, you believe every word another says. You take on the shape of their words unresisting. Like the still pond you reflect their reality back to them. Such is love. You become water poured into a glass, a vessel, a pitcher. Sometimes the other will hate what they see. They plunge their spears into you, but they seek only to destroy their own reflection. You are the pond, the river; you remain unaltered by their attacks.

Presence is the deep listening of the ocean, an unfathomable listening. Presence is the reception of frequencies unseen and unheard by the eye, the ear, the mind. With presence your body vibrates with opening. It becomes a receiver for the truth that shivers beneath words, beneath appearances, beneath thought.

Whisper to water and drink in your truth. Look into water and see yourself as you were created. Become water and you will know presence.

Visualization for Embodying Presence

Prepare your space; find somewhere quiet and comfortable where you will not be disturbed. This is your time, just for you, to rest and connect

Sit or lie comfortably. Close your eyes and breathe deeply. Follow the silken stream of your breath as it flows into your lungs. This air around you is infused with light. As you bring it into your lungs, it disperses through your body. The light you breathe is intelligent. It brings healing and nourishment to each of the different parts of your body, giving every cell exactly what it needs. Notice how your lungs become empty as you exhale. Notice a feeling of relaxation and wellbeing as you become empty of breath, and then effortlessly filled again.

Allow your eyes to relax. Feel the muscles around your eyes relaxing and letting go. Allow your jaw and tongue to relax. Let your limbs become pleasantly heavy. A pleasantly warm energy begins to flow up your body, emanating from the Earth. As it flows through your body, it feels as though each part of your body is expanding beyond your physical dimensions. The energy washes into your feet, and your toes uncurl and expand. The muscles of your calves expand, your knees feel light and spacious. The energy washes up your thighs, your hips and lower back, waves of soft light washing tension and worry from the muscles around your spine, your jaw, your face, your forehead, your eyes, your crown. A wave of relaxation cascading down your shoulders, your arms, flowing out your fingertips. Feel your body tingling, letting go, and taking on new dimensions.

A shimmering, diamond-bright pyramid rises around and above you. It glints with gold and tourmaline, moonstone, and amethyst. It holds you in an inviolable field of calm protection. Within this pyramid, there is only truth. You are safe and cared for, and all of your needs are met. Rest in this feeling for a moment, of being safe and cared for, of knowing that all of your needs are, and always will be, met.

(Deep breath)

A golden vortex opens before you, rotating slowly, rising through the top of the pyramid. It is a divine portal, ready to remove anything you no longer want to carry. Anything you place into this vortex will disappear from your life forever.

Purse your lips and breathe out slowly, but with some force, as if blowing out a row of candles. You will take five deep breaths this way.

With the first exhale, watch any remaining tension flowing out from all of your muscles. The tension leaves on the breath and is sent into the golden vortex, taken far, far away, never to return. Without thinking, without trying, simply notice what it looks like as it leaves you. Notice any sensations, memories, or thoughts that surface as you let it go.

With your second exhale, watch the excess fire and sparks of your nervous system flowing out on your stream of breath. Without thinking, without trying, notice what it looks like as it leaves you. This sparking energy streams directly into the vortex and is carried far, far away, never to return.

With your third exhale, watch as all density and stuckness lodged in all of your cells unlodges and flows out on the stream of your breath. Without thinking, without trying, notice what it looks like as it leaves you. This energy streams directly into the vortex and is carried far, far away, never to return.

With your fourth exhale, watch as all of the thoughts and stories of the outside world gather in one reservoir and then flow out on the stream of your breath. Without thinking, without trying, notice what it looks like as it leaves you. This energy streams directly into the vortex and is carried far, far away, never to return.

With your final breath, let anything that is still left within you, anything you still want to let go of, come out on the stream of your breath. You do not have to know what it is; simply let it go. Without thinking, without trying, notice what it looks like as it leaves you. This energy streams directly into the vortex and is carried far, far away, never to return.

The vortex gently closes up, disappearing into a tiny pinprick of light. Then, all becomes dark and still.

Take a moment to rest in your body and notice the effect of this release. Feel the shape and dimensions of your body.

(Pause and witness)

Find yourself standing in a dark, cool place. It is very, very early morning, just before dawn. The stars and moon have receded, and there is nothing but a welcoming darkness. You can hear water rushing nearby, a stream. Your skin tingles with pleasure and aliveness in this predawn quiet.

The ground beneath your feet is pleasantly cool and soft, fragrant and rich. It smells of damp soil. As you stand on this soft, cool Earth, you can feel it cradling the bottoms of your feet. The Earth seems to hug your feet, sending a healing, relaxing energy into your whole body through the sensitive reflexology points of the soles of your feet. Mother Nature is giving you a foot massage! You take a step on the cool earth, and another. With each step, the ground rises to meet you, softly cradling your tender foot. The Earth sends energy up your legs, through your knees, into your back and spine, shoulders and neck, aligning, straightening, and balancing your musculature from the ground up. You know instinctively that, though it is still dark, it is safe and pleasurable to walk on this ground. There is nothing hard or sharp that will hurt you. The ground itself emanates pure love and healing, bringing you everything you need simply by walking.

You feel into a new knowing- that the Earth is your mother and that your body is made of Earth. Your mother knows your body, inside and out. She knows exactly what you need at all times and will take care of you always. You feel your heart opening to receive this truth deep, deep into the cells of your body.

As you stand, receiving loving, living care of the Earth mother, the dawn begins to lighten the sky. Your surroundings resolve themselves from the darkness. You can see the silhouettes of tall pine trees, their trunks glowing as though overlaid with pearl, dark evergreen needles limned in silver.

To your left you see a stream flowing, gentle eddies and currents form playful spirals that curl and ripple. As the sun rises its rays infuse the water with flecks of gold, rose, diamond, and amethyst winking and glittering from the clear depths. The bed of the stream is cushioned with soft sand and smooth stones.

Naked, you slip into the water. It cradles your body with invigorating coolness. The water is soft against your body, softer than any water you have ever felt. You lay back in the soft, cool stream and watch the sun rise in the distance. It sends golden rays out over the sky, brightening the clouds and gilding the land around you in liquid gold. You can feel your body begin to glow bronze and rosy and vital in the dawn.

You look down at the water and realize it is infused with light. The water is, in fact, more light than matter. You watch as dark, dense energies detach from your body, flowing out from your muscles and cells. You see this energy floating downstream, sloughed from of you by the flowing, loving water. The dense energies are carried away from you. You can see them- dark gray plasma and smoke. Take time to release all that is heavy and dead within you.

(Pause)

Now you submerge yourself and realize you can breathe this water. Your whole body is submerged, and you breathe comfortably. As you breathe, the water infuses your lungs and heart with radiant white light, cleansing you gently of grief and heartache.

(Pause to release)

You feel density flow out of the muscles in your face and jaw, your throat. Feel the water cleansing and illuminating your hair and skin, washing away all blemishes so that you become radiant, bright, and full of joy. The water washes into your brain, and you feel it cool and loving, releasing thoughtforms of fear and worry, blame and judgment.

(Pause to release)

Coming back to the surface, you cup your hands and drink. The water is sweet and cool, like nectar. As you drink, you bring the light of the water into all of your cells. Your body is so thirsty for this water, so you drink and drink and drink. Drink all you need.

The liquid light permeates your body from the inside out. Nothing dense, dark, heavy, or dead can survive in your body now. You become radiant with light, and any viruses, parasites, or waste that vibrates at a level lower than love is flows out from your body. Let yourself gently release whatever needs to come out- through your pores, your bowels, your breath. You release it all comfortably and without fear or shame into the infinitely soft and loving water. The water is an invitation to let go completely, an invitation your body has been waiting for so very long.

Rest here, floating in the water for as long as you need.

(Long pause to rest and release)

Now the water communicates that it wants to bring you somewhere. You close your eyes and let it wrap you in a soft, warm cocoon, as soft and comfortable as a cloud. This cloud acts like a little boat, and as it wraps around you, warm and soft, you feel yourself relaxing into trust. The little cloudboat enters into the water's current, and you float downstream, being rocked like a baby in a cradle by the swirling eddies. Allow yourself to express any tones or sounds that arise as you float.

(Pause, rest, and express)

You now feel your cloudboat being lifted out of the water and placed on a firm surface. The cloud dissolves around you and you sit up.

The darkness lifts, and you find yourself sitting on a small, sturdy raft. All around you, as far as you can see is a vast ocean, stretching to the horizon and beyond. You turn in a 360 circle and realize you are completely surrounded by water, boundless and eternal, spreading in every direction as far as you can see. You are unafraid, sitting on this raft.

The water is completely, utterly still, not one ripple along its surface. The world echoes with silence, a deeper silence than you have ever experienced. The silence is welcoming, but palpable. You can feel the smooth weight of it on your skin. It is as though the silence is a deep, inner ear, listening and responsive to your every movement.

Experimentally, you express a single tone, a note, or a word. Let it arise from the depths of you, and express it out loud, into the silence.

Immediately, a ripple extends in 360 degrees, originating from where you sit on your small, sturdy raft. You see the ripple, a perfect reflection of the frequency of your voice, creating an ever-larger circle in the otherwise tranquil water, extending toward the horizon in all directions. You know that this ripple will go on forever, vibrating for eternity in the quantum field.

You gradually come to understand that you are sitting in the exact center of your own throat chakra, and that every word you speak cannot help but send ripples into this vast ocean of the universe.

You sit on your raft and contemplate this understanding. What does it mean to you?

(Pause and reflect)

Presently you see, coming toward you, a bright, golden light, shot through with deep, royal blue. It comes closer and closer and resolves into the form of a beautiful light-being, gliding toward you on outstretched golden-blue wings. It is Archangel Michael coming toward you, the keeper of the throat chakra of humanity, and the universal, angelic guide for clear, loving, honest, and authentic communication. As he alights next to you on the sturdy platform, he transmits his energy of calm dignity, unshakable courage, devotion, and deep, abiding truth. You rest in silence with him, receiving his divine masculine transmission of love.

Archangel Michael has a message for you. There is a truth you have been too afraid to acknowledge, but it is now time to bring it into your conscious awareness. This is a healing truth, and your soul is ready for it to come to light. Archangel Michael assures you that any and all resources will be provided for the resolution of any disruption this truth may cause in your life. You turn to look into his firm, loving gaze, and you know that he is stronger than any fear. He will never abandon you to the consequences of this truth but will support you in every way as you acknowledge it. He loves you and is devoted to you, and he will not rest until your healing is complete.

Let yourself sink back into presence, where there is no fear, only loving receptivity, and allow this truth to surface. Speak it out loud into the gentle, boundless water of your existence. Trust in the words you speak.

(Long pause for speaking and listening to truth)

It is now time to bring this truth into your waking life. Keeping your eyes closed, become aware of your physical body. Bring movement into your fingers, your toes, your ankles, your shoulders. With eyes still closed, raise your right hand, and gently but firmly tap your sternum several times to imprint this truth into your body. You may be tempted to deny it later. Set the intention now to believe in every word you said, in every insight that came to you.

Still resting in the presence of this loving truth, and Archangel Michael's undying devotion, allow your eyes to open. Remain this way for a few moments as you take in your surroundings.

And gradually, when you're ready, move back into your waking life.

Before you engage in any practical tasks, take time to journal, write, or create a voice recording to reflect on what you experienced. Note how you feel, and what has changed for you. This act of reflection will even more firmly imprint the experience into your body.

Chapter 7: Trust

Teachings of Trust

Watch as fire erupts from the center of the heart of the phoenix. Watch as flames wrap around the proud, blazing feathers and the hooked beak. The phoenix gives itself over to its own immolation. A fire without smoke. An immaculate conflagration. The eyes are the only things that do not flicker.

This is not the fire of purification, it is not the burning of things that are heavy, as the phoenix is flame incarnate. Fire is the nature of the phoenix. It is born in flame and lives in blazing radiance. Its death is simply the final expression of its truest form.

Watch as the fire cascades upwards, rising finally into realms unseen. It leaves behind not ash, not feathers, not soot, but diamonds. Glittering dust, the ash of celestial transformation.

In the center of the diamond nest stirs a small, naked form, shivering in the cold left behind from the departing conflagration.

How shocking, this rebirth. How unexpected! We imagine the phoenix reborn, rising proud and strong from the ashes, wings outstretched, ready to command the wind. Instead we see, born from the transmuting fire, this small and tender thing. Naked wings flap feebly, the beak too large, too heavy for the skinny neck. And yet, even now its eyes do not flicker.

Such is trust. To give up all you have ever known. To let go, again and again of your strength, your power, your form, to be reborn into something tiny and weak and unrecognizable. And to know, utterly, that this moment is your strongest yet.

Joy will creep into the space behind your eyes like the slow fingers of the rising dawn. Love will nestle softly into your heart while you are looking elsewhere. These forces will be unrecognizable to you. You will want to shove them away. You will be afraid to welcome them, afraid they are simply visiting, that they are just stopping by, that they will leave you again more bereft than before.

You fear that they will vanish like smoke, like all of the good things that have come to you, that seemed too good to be true and were.

And yet, the phoenix-even as he sits at the mercy of the world, his eyes do not flicker. He knows that love, that joy- he knows that these are the only real, the only constant things. He has staked his life on it.

Visualization for Embodying Trust

Prepare your space; find somewhere quiet and comfortable where you will not be disturbed. This is your time, just for you, to rest and connect. You may want to have a pen and paper at hand for this visualization.

Sit or lie comfortably. Close your eyes and breathe deeply. Follow the silken stream of your breath as it flows into your lungs. This air around you is infused with light. As you bring it into your lungs, it disperses through your body. The light you breathe is intelligent, and it effortlessly delivers healing and nourishment to each of the different parts of your body, giving every cell exactly what it needs.

Allow your eyes to relax. Feel the muscles around your eyes relaxing and letting go. Allow your jaw and tongue to relax. Let your limbs become pleasantly heavy. A pleasantly warm energy begins to flow up your body, emanating from the Earth. As it flows through your body, it feels as though each part of your body is expanding beyond your physical dimensions. The energy washes into your feet, and your toes uncurl and expand. The muscles of your calves expand, your knees feel light and spacious. The energy washes up your thighs, your hips and lower back, waves of soft light washing tension and worry from the muscles around your spine, your jaw, your face, your forehead, your eyes, your crown. A wave of relaxation cascading down your shoulders, your arms, flowing out your fingertips. Feel your body tingling, letting go, and taking on new dimensions.

A shimmering, diamond-bright pyramid rises around and above you. It glints with gold and tourmaline, moonstone, sapphire, ruby and amethyst. It holds you in an inviolable field of calm protection. Within this pyramid, there is only truth. You are safe and cared for, and all of your needs are met. Rest in this feeling for a moment, of being safe and cared for, of knowing that all of your needs are, and always will be, met.

(Pause and rest)

A golden vortex opens before you, rotating slowly, rising through the top of the pyramid. It is a divine portal, ready to remove anything you no longer want to carry. Anything you place into this vortex will disappear from your life forever.

Purse your lips and breathe out slowly, but with some force, as if blowing out a row of candles. You will take five deep breaths this way.

With the first exhale, watch any remaining tension flowing out from all of your muscles. The tension leaves on the breath and is sent into the golden vortex, taken far, far away, never to return. Without thinking, without trying, simply notice what it looks like as it leaves you. Notice any sensations, memories, or thoughts that surface as you let it go.

With your second exhale, watch the excess fire and sparks of your nervous system flowing out on your stream of breath. Without thinking, without trying, notice what it looks like as it leaves you. This sparking energy streams directly into the vortex and is carried far, far away, never to return.

With your third exhale, watch as all density and stuckness lodged in all of your cells unlodges and flows out on the stream of your breath. Without thinking, without trying, notice what it looks like as it leaves you. This energy streams directly into the vortex and is carried far, far away, never to return.

With your fourth exhale, watch as all of the thoughts and stories of the outside world gather in one reservoir and then flow out on the stream of your breath. Without thinking, without trying, notice what it looks like as it leaves you. This energy streams directly into the vortex and is carried far, far away, never to return.

With your final breath, let anything that is still left within you, anything you still want to let go of, come out on the stream of your breath. You do not have to know what it is; simply let it go. Without thinking, without trying, notice what it looks like as it leaves you. This energy streams directly into the vortex and is carried far, far away, never to return.

The vortex gently closes up, disappearing into a tiny pinprick of light. Then, all becomes dark and still.

Take a moment to rest in your body and notice the effect of this release. Feel the shape and dimensions of your body.

(Pause and notice)

You become aware that you are walking along a high mountain pass. The sun shines above you in a cheerful sky blue, as a bluebird's wing. Snow glitters all around you like diamonds. You scoop it up in your hands and become aware that you are holding diamond dust, precious and beautiful and alive with the rays of the sun. Joyfully you toss it in the air above you and watch it cascade downward onto you, a shower of adamantine light, settling in your hair and clothes as sparkling, glittering dust. Though there is snow, you are not cold. You walk now, sparkling more brightly than the snow itself. The diamond dust activates joy in the center of your heart and forms a blazing aureole of protection around your body.

You look around and as far as you can see there are bright mountaintops, covered in snow and glinting with hints of rose and azure, emerald and aquamarine in the sunshine. It is peaceful here, and quiet.

Soon, you come upon a wide gorge and see that the path ends here. You look down, far, far below you can see a river, thin as a thread and so far down the sound of its massive crashing floats up, soft as a whisper. You look up, and across the cavern you can see the small, dark opening of a cave. There is something precious for you in that cave. Every fiber of your being resonates with joy and anticipation at the thought of what you are to receive in that cave.

You see that the aureole of protection is swirling around you, emanating from your open and loving heart. You know, deep in your cells, that you are safe and that there is absolutely nothing to fear. Smiling, and without hesitation, you step over the rim of the cavern, placing your foot onto what looks like thin air.

Immediately a large stone forms underneath your foot, holding you firmly and safely, far, far above the river below. You take a deep breath, bring your other foot off of the ground, and step it in front of you. Immediately another stone forms beneath that foot. You are now standing on two stones, safe and held, high above the ground below.

You feel a sense of lightness and freedom overtake you as you begin to understand how unconditionally safe and held you are. Experimentally you leap sideways into thin air. A stone forms underneath you as you land, firm and unmoving. You lose your balance, however, and fall. In the moment you think you may plunge downward, a soft, fluffy cloud forms underneath you and catches you. You laugh, wrapped in its feathery softness.

You stand again and look up. The cave is waiting!

Excited, you dance, skip, jump, run across the cavern. With each footfall, a firm stone forms beneath, creating a bridge just the shape of your journey. Take a moment to move over the gorge in any way that feels good to you.

(Pause to cross the cavern)

You reach the other side of the cavern and step onto the waiting path. Turn and look. What does the path look like over the gorge? What was your route? Was it straight and clean or sporadic and impetuous? What pattern have the stones made in your wake?

(Pause to notice)

You wave your hand, and the bridge disappears. You no longer need it. The air become still and clear again, the void above the gorge becoming a clean slate awaiting your next journey across.

Turning around again, you behold the opening of the cave. It forms an archway just your size. You are not certain if there is enough space to enter without stooping. Stones line the outside of the entrance. At the apex, just above eye level, a symbol or glyph is carved into the stone. What does it look like? Take a moment to look, without thinking or analyzing.

(Pause to look)

You understand that this is the name of your soul, inscribed in light language above the entrance to this cave.

If you like, you can take a moment to open your eyes and, maintaining the connection to your inner eye, draw what you see. When finished, settle back in and take a few deep breaths, returning to the entrance of the cave.

(Pause to draw or absorb the symbol)

Each time you come back to the entrance here, know that this glyph may transform or reveal more of itself.

Now you peer into the cave, but you can see only darkness. You take a deep breath and walk confidently through the entrance with your head held high. The archway raises as you enter, expanding instantaneously to accommodate your height.

You stand just inside the cave. All is dark. You turn to look behind you. The entrance you just came through is bright and clear, and through the archway you can see mountains rising in the distance. But you understand the light from the outside cannot penetrate here.

You look down at your hands and see that they are glowing, luminescent. Your whole body still sparkles and glows with the inviolable, unconditional protection that emanates from your effortlessly confident and joyful heart. You look up and, in the darkness, behold the shape of your energy field. With every heartbeat, the veins that form the sacred geometry of your energy field pulse with golden light. It is your own inner light that illumines the cave. Soon, your eyes become accustomed to the dimness. Notice what it looks like here in this cave. Take time to explore.

(Pause to explore)

Gradually, you become aware of a dark tunnel at the back of the cave. There is a light slowly approaching toward you from within the tunnel. This is a light unlike any you've ever seen. It is deep, cobalt blue, glittering with dark, silver specks, like small shooting stars.

A figure steps out from the mouth of the tunnel. You behold the dark cloak. It is not fabric, but a swirling cloak made of void, of nothingness. A hood covers the head and face, and you see the glittering diamond scythe in its hand.

Taking a deep breath, knowing you are still held in the inviolable protection of your inner light, you smile and welcome Death.

He pulls the hood back from his head, revealing a skull, breathtaking in its beauty. Softly iridescent, it glows with pearlescent rose, azure, and delicate violet shades.

From the safe and fearless space of your glittering energy field, you stand and behold Death, face to face. Allow some time for any emotions, images, thoughts, or memories to surface.

(Long pause to witness)

Death regards you steadily, emanating unconditional love. In him, you recognize an old, old friend whom you have met many times before.

With your inviolable free will, Death cannot approach any closer unless you invite him to. He bows, however, and communicates that he has a gift for you.

Death brings the gift of finality, of irreversible change. He sees that you are holding onto something, or perhaps many things, that you are ready to release for good. He sees that, while they once served a purpose, they no longer serve you, and that they are drawing life force from what truly matters in your life. He invites you to place these heavy things into his hands. Once you give them over, they will not be able to return to you.

Perhaps this is a habit, an addiction, a thought pattern, a story, a relationship, an agreement, a contract, a recurring situation, or a karmic loop that you have tried to release many times without success. Death stands before you now in unconditional love and strength, offering the opportunity to release this thing, or these many things, once and for all.

Take the time you need to remove all you would like to release forever from your life and place it all into the welcoming hands of Death. Take time as well for any emotions to surface as you do this. You may feel relief, fear, grief, anger. Let it all come up and flow into the loving, infinite hands of Death.

(Long pause for conscious release)

Death brings all you have given him beneath the dark void of his cloak, where it vanishes instantly. He bows again, sending you vibrations of gratitude, love, and pride for your courage in releasing these things from your life, into his capable hands. Then, turning, he disappears back down the tunnel. You watch him go, a cobalt light swirling with dark silver. You watch until he disappears into the darkness, taking with him all that was heavy.

You turn around now and behold the bright, sunlit entrance of the cave behind you. You become aware that the cave itself has become drenched in sunlight. Golden rays flow in through the open archway, which has expanded in size and rises far, far above your head. Every aspect of the cave is limned in golden light, glowing and gilded. You can see the whole landscape from where you stand, mountains rising far in the distance, their peaks covered in snow, flashing with ruby and coral, sapphire, and hints of burnt orange under the blazing sun.

You step back out of the cave, standing on the path that leads back to the gorge. Notice how your body feels now, bathed in the light of the sun, free from all that you have let go of.

(Long pause to witness)

It is now time to bring this feeling into your waking life. Breathe deeply, bringing this feeling into your lungs, into your belly, into your heart. Keeping your eyes closed, become aware of your physical body. Bring movement into your fingers, your toes, your ankles, your shoulders. With eyes still closed, raise your right hand, and gently but firmly tap your sternum, and anywhere else that feels good, several times to imprint these feelings of lightness, freedom, and safety into your body. Know that your courage and trust has set catalytic changes into motion.

Still resting in presence, open your eyes. Remain this way for a few moments as you take in your surroundings.

And gradually, when you're ready, move back into your waking life.

Before you engage in any practical tasks, take time to journal, write, or create a voice recording to reflect on what you experienced. Note how you feel, and what has changed for you. This act of reflection will even more firmly imprint the experience into your body.

Chapter 6: Sovereignty

Teachings of Sovereignty

"It's a rock," he said.
And walked away.

In a burst of laughter, sudden as sunshine,
Joyful as breaking glass,

I got the joke.

The absurdity of our suffering.
How we drape our simple existence
in solemn, ponderous concatenations of truth and meaning.
Layer upon layer of convincing ourselves of our own significance.
How funny- when we're already here, always and eternally arriving.

    And yet,
    And yet.

This seeking:
It's the flesh around the spine.
The greatest story ever told.

Why create anything if the universe is meaningless?
Ask this of the artist and
He looks at you, irritated.
He tries to send you away.

    Because it's beautiful.

Because it brings me joy.
Because I wanted to see if I could.

Ask this of the holy man and he says,
"why do you breathe?"

Why? Why? Why?

Why not?

In this way we see
the true precursor to creation
Is a shrug.

The master craftsman absorbed in his work doesn't give thought to "meaning" or "purpose" or "outcome."
He creates because his hands move in the process of creation.

And so, all of life becomes tautology:
I do because I do.
I am because, therefore, and so
I AM

The I AM a waterfall of grace- nothing can cling to it.
Not even us.

We get trapped because it's fun to forget.
And it's fun to remember again.

Oh yes. It's just a race.
Just a game.
Just a painting.

Just a child.
Just a life.

    And yet,
    And yet.

In this moment
It's my whole world.

--

    Beyond blame, beyond criticism, beyond judgement, beyond victimhood: there is sovereignty. Void over void, such is sovereignty. Using it, the noble-minded cannot use it. The noble-minded can only become it.
    In this becoming, the noble-minded command the Earth, the Cosmos, the air and fire and water and sea, but never lift a hand to do so.

Visualization for Embodying Sovereignty

Prepare your space; find somewhere quiet and comfortable where you will not be disturbed. This is your time, just for you, to rest and connect.

Sit or lie comfortably. Close your eyes and breathe deeply. Follow the quiet stream of your breath as it flows into your lungs. Feel as your chest rises and falls, slowing into its natural rhythm. Feel your belly relax. Feel the muscles around the base of your spine and let them relax completely.

The air around you is infused with light. As you bring it into your lungs, it disperses through your body. The light you breathe is intelligent, and it effortlessly delivers healing and nourishment to each of the different parts of your body, giving every organ exactly what it needs. It irradiates your skin, bringing a glow to your whole body.

Allow your eyes to relax. Feel the muscles around your eyes relaxing and letting go. Allow your jaw and tongue to relax. Let your limbs become pleasantly heavy. A pleasant, warm energy begins to flow up your body, emanating from the Earth. As it flows through your body, it feels as though each part of your body is expanding beyond your physical dimensions. The energy washes into your feet, and your toes uncurl and expand. Feel the muscles of your calves expand, your knees feel light and spacious. The energy washes up your thighs, your hips and lower back, waves of soft light washing tension and worry from the muscles around your spine, your jaw, your face, your forehead, your eyes, your crown. A wave of relaxation cascades down your shoulders, your arms, flowing out your fingertips. Feel your body tingling, letting go, and taking on new dimensions.

A shimmering, diamond-bright pyramid rises around and above you. It glints with gold and tourmaline, moonstone, sapphire, ruby, and amethyst. You are now held in a field of calm protection.

You are safe and cared for, and all of your needs are met. Rest in this feeling for a moment, of being safe and cared for, of knowing that all of your needs are, and always will be, met.

    A golden vortex opens before you, rotating slowly, rising through the top of the pyramid. It is a divine portal, ready to remove anything you no longer want to carry.

    Purse your lips and breathe out slowly, but with some force, as if blowing out a row of candles. You will take five deep breaths this way.

    With the first exhale, watch any remaining tension flowing out from all of your muscles. The tension leaves on the breath and is sent into the golden vortex, taken far, far away, never to return. Without thinking, without trying, simply notice what it looks like as it leaves you. Notice any sensations, memories, or thoughts that surface as you let it go.

    With your second exhale, watch the excess fire and sparks of your nervous system flowing out on your stream of breath. Without thinking, without trying, notice what it looks like as it leaves you. This sparking energy streams directly into the vortex and is carried far, far away, never to return.

    With your third exhale, watch as all density and stuckness lodged in all of your cells unsticks and flows out on the stream of your breath. Without thinking, without trying, notice what it looks like as it leaves you. This energy streams directly into the vortex and is carried far, far away, never to return.

    With your fourth exhale, watch as all of the thoughts and stories of the outside world gather into one reservoir within you, and then flow out on the stream of your breath. Without thinking, without trying, notice what it looks like as it leaves you. This energy streams directly into the vortex and is carried far, far away, never to return.

With your final breath, let anything that is still left within you, anything you still want to let go of, come out on the stream of your breath. You do not have to know what it is; simply let it go. Without thinking, without trying, notice what it looks like as it leaves you. This energy streams directly into the vortex and is carried far, far away, never to return.

The vortex gently closes up, disappearing into a tiny pinprick of light. Then, all becomes dark and still.

Take a moment to rest in your body and notice the effect of this release.

(Pause and rest)

You gradually become aware that you are standing in a spacious, sun-drenched room. The ceilings are vaulted, and fine, mellow wooden beams arch high above your head. The room is beautiful, orderly, and balanced, furnished in exquisite taste, just to your liking. Look around. What does it look like? Walk around the room for a moment and notice. You may pick up objects, feel their texture and weight. This is your room and everything in it is yours.

(Pause to explore)

In your tour of the room, you walk past a full-length mirror and catch sight of your reflection. There is a crown on your head, and you are wearing robes of the finest woven cloth. As you study your reflection, you realize that you are the highest royalty in the land, the queen or king of a vast domain. Contemplate your reflection for a moment. What do you look like? What are you wearing? Is your clothing simple or opulent? What does the crown look like? Are you wearing jewels or gemstones? Take a moment to behold your sovereign self.

(Pause and witness)

You become aware of a rumble of sound and realize it is coming from outside. You notice there are large, clear double-doors leading out onto a stone balcony. The stone of the balcony is a soft rose cream, glowing in the sunlight. As you approach the doors, they swing open on their own and you can hear the roar of a crowd. You step out onto the balcony and behold your kingdom.

Verdant hills undulate in every direction, smudged with the darker jade of evergreen forests. A bright sky, blue as a robin's egg arches overhead, wide and bright. The sun shines golden bright, illuminating the land in loving majesty.

Below you is a spacious, stone courtyard lined with gardens on every side. It is silent and still. As you look around, you notice a large, slate-stone wall rising around the perimeter of your castle. It is heavy and dark, blighting the view of the landscape. Through narrow gates that punctuate the wall at intervals, you can see masses of people clustered. Many, many people, are there, their hands reaching through the gates, crying out. You know at once that these are your people, the people of the land, and that they are in need. Compassion fills your heart.

Closing your eyes, you summon a bright, iridescent bubble, which appears in front of you. You step into the bubble, and your robes suddenly glow the purest white. The bubble brings you down into the courtyard, gently dissolving as you land. You can feel the white blaze of energy remaining around your body, radiating brighter than the sun. As you step through the courtyard, you feel a warm glow deep, deep within you, so deep it is not contained in your physical body. It comes from somewhere you cannot know, a still and silent space ungoverned by any laws you have ever known.

From this deep, dark space, a slow spiral emerges, glinting a lustrous silver. It winds its way from this unfathomable place, spiraling up your body and out the top of your crowned head. You understand that this slow, immeasurable force is your own divine will. As it continues to spiral through you, emanating from your deepest self, it clears away all fear and doubt. You feel a sense of power, lightness, and wellbeing overtake you. Rest for a moment in this feeling of power, lightness, and wellbeing.

(Pause and notice)

You step toward the tall, forbidding wall. Through a narrow gate you see many, many people crying out. They have needs that have not been met. Needs for shelter and warmth, nourishment and compassion.

As you look upon them, you realize that each person beyond the wall is an aspect of your own self. They comprise the many, many parts of *you* that make up your being. You see that so many of these parts have been neglected, shut out, and denied, and they are here, crying for attention.

From the unfathomable depths, the place from where your divine will emanates, you lift one hand with loving intention.

Immediately the heavy, dark, forbidding wall lifts into the air. As it floats above, the sun pours golden light on it, washing away the darkness and heaviness, revealing soft, mellow rose-gold stone underneath. You wave your hand and the wall breaks apart, still floating above you. With one final flick of your wrist, the wall reforms into beautiful, lovely stone houses that float downwards and come to rest, nestled within the verdant hills of the land.

You turn to the people, the people who are you, and see that there is no barrier any longer between you and them. You declare in ringing tones that each and every one of them shall have their needs met, immediately and from now on, unconditionally and without question.

You see up close the aspects of self- the inner child and inner mother, the inner father. The inner creator, the inner beggar. The inner slave. The innocent, the artist, the explorer and the wise one, the sage and the jester. The prostitute and the murderer. The weakling and the predator. All are here within your kingdom. Which ones do you still deny? Which ones are you tempted to leave in darkness? Which ones do you condemn? Pause to make peace with these aspects of self.

(Pause and receive peace)

You turn and walk back up the courtyard and up the steps of your castle. In the very heart of your castle is a throne, in a large, light-filled room. This is the throne of the heart, your rightful place. You walk up three marble steps and take your seat on the throne.

There is someone to see you. An aspect of self that has needs that haven't been met. Still radiating blazing white light, seated on the compassionate throne of your loving heart, safe and protected, and feeling the slow, strong spiral of your divine will rising eternally within, you beckon them forward.

What aspect of self comes to you now in need and humble supplication? What are they asking for? Listen. You promise you will give them all that they need from now on.

(Long pause to listen)

Perhaps another aspect of self comes forward now. What are they asking for? Listen.

(Long pause and listen)

You promise you will give them all that they need from now on.

With each promise you make, the spiral of your divine will becomes stronger, clearer, and more tangible. The energy field of sparkling white light surrounding you becomes larger and even brighter, until you are almost too radiant to look upon. Behold yourself now.

You are not finished, however. Something tugs at your memory, a feeling of something forgotten, something left undone.

All at once, you remember.

Standing, you turn and walk toward a small, thick, oaken door at the back of the room. It opens as you approach, revealing a dark set of stone, spiral stairs, descending downwards into the bowels of your castle. The air around the stairway is black as pitch, but as you step through the door, the white light blazing from your heart and around your body lights the causeway like a firework. You descend the stairs as a walking star.

Down, down you go, penetrating into the deepest regions of the castle. As you descend, the air becomes heavy, thick, and dense. Here is gathered the long-suppressed energy of shame that clogs the bowels of your being. The shame presses on you, but it cannot touch the effortless and inviolable white light of your energy field. You are completely safe, protected, and powerful, cutting a swath of light through the density. You breathe easily within your star of light.

Take a moment to descend deeper and deeper into your own depths, breathing light into the darkness.

(Pause and breathe)

Finally, you reach the very bottom stair. Ahead of you is a single, barred door. It has not been opened for a very long time. This is where you house your deepest shame. Whatever is within the cell stirs as it feels the light of your presence for the first time. The bars rattle, and you can hear harsh sounds of breathing.

Slowly, your heart breaking open with compassion, you approach the door. You reach into your pocket and find a key, one you had placed there long ago. You grasp it in long, luminous fingers and fit it into the keyhole. With a powerful, decisive hand you turn the key and fling open the door.

The blazing light of your breaking, compassionate heart spills into the dark cell. What, or whom, do you behold there?

Witness it now with the inviolable eyes of compassion. Let it speak to you for as long as you need it to.

(Long pause to witness)

When this part of you is done speaking, you gather the figure into your shining, lustrous arms and hold it close. Years and years of dirt, grime, and filth stream off of it, revealing its true form. What does it look like, in the light of your compassion?

As you hold the figure close to you, radiating light and love, you understand that all is forgiven. All is forgiven. All is forgiven.

(Pause and notice what it feels like to be entirely and eternally forgiven).

Still holding the figure to your heart, you summon another gleaming, iridescent bubble. It forms around you both and lifts you into the sun-drenched courtyard of your castle.

As the bubble dissolves, you let go of the figure and watch it stand upright, tall, and strong in the sun. You promise to check in on this figure every day for the next week to make sure it has everything it needs. You promise to give it everything it needs, without condition. This is a sacred vow, and as you speak it, the white starlight of your presence gleams even brighter than the sun.

The figure walks away from you, radiating its own aura of love.

(Long pause to witness)

It is now time to bring this feeling into your waking life. Breathing deeply, you bring the white light of power, strength, dignity, and fearlessness into your lungs, into your belly, and into your heart. White starlight irradiates every cell of your body.

Keeping your eyes closed, become aware of your physical body. Bring movement into your fingers, your toes, your ankles, your shoulders. With eyes still closed, raise your right hand, and gently but firmly tap your sternum, and anywhere else that feels good, to imprint these feelings into your body.

Still resting in this feeling of power and freedom, open your eyes. Remain this way for a few moments as you take in your surroundings.

And gradually, when you're ready, move back into your waking life.

Before you engage in any practical tasks, take time to journal, write, or create a voice recording to reflect on what you experienced. Note how you feel, and what has changed for you. This act of reflection will even more firmly imprint the experience into your body.

Chapter 9: Devotion

Teachings of Devotion

At the center of your heart lives your deepest longing. It was planted in you, a divine seed of salvation. It is the one thing more compelling than your fears. It is the origin of your devotion. Once you touch it, it grows. It brims over- an eternal wellspring at the center of your heart.

With devotion comes worship. As your devotion leads you from darkness, you discover that only the divine knows how to worship. You discover that, in worshipping, you become divine.

As you worship- the tree, the ant, the spider, the flawed and quaking man at your feet- you find, that the only force large enough to house your devotion is God itself. Your devotion is bigger than you, the biggest force you could conceive of: the only force that could conceive of *you*. Devotion is relentless. It expands you beyond your boundaries until you break. You breathe, and you break again. You break until you have no choice but to become divine. It the only thing that breaks without shattering.

You have given and given and given. You stand with empty hands. You gnash your teeth at the ingratitude, the ways that you have been brushed aside in your giving, at the ways your worship has been crushed in the hands and minds of those who would possess it. You have loved and been broken, and you have broken again. You have offered yourself up for this breaking. You have given and given. You have thrown your light before swine. You have been drained to emptiness. You declare, fists raised, that you will not love again this undeserving world.

And then, to your dismay and, yes, wry amusement, the love rises again unbidden. It flows through your skin, your pores. It emanates from you, involuntary as breath. You cannot help it. You are helpless in the face of it. You watch this light trickling from your body. You finally accept that you are love, and all else falls away.

    You remember suddenly that love and all of its acts are eternally reclaimed, just as water draws back into the sky to become rain. You understand that no act of love is ever wasted. You remember that all you have given has fallen on fertile ground: your devotion like fallen rain on the garden of Earth, nourishing the flowing, flourishing, unheeding garden of your eternal and sacred heart.

Visualization for Embodying Devotion

Prepare your space; find somewhere quiet and comfortable where you will not be disturbed. This is your time, just for you, to rest and connect.

Sit or lay comfortably. Close your eyes and breathe deeply. Follow the quiet stream of your breath as it flows into your lungs. Feel as your chest rises and falls, slowing into its natural rhythm. Feel your belly relax. Feel the muscles around the base of your spine and let them relax completely.

The air around you is infused with light. As you bring it into your lungs, it disperses through your body. The light you breathe is intelligent, and it effortlessly delivers healing and nourishment to each of the different parts of your body, giving every organ exactly what it needs. It irradiates your skin, bringing a glow to your whole body.

Allow your eyes to relax. Feel the muscles around your eyes relaxing and letting go. Allow your jaw and tongue to relax. Let your limbs become pleasantly heavy. A pleasantly warm energy begins to flow up your body, emanating from the Earth. As it flows through your body, it feels as though each part of your body is expanding beyond your physical dimensions. The energy washes into your feet, and your toes uncurl and expand. The muscles of your calves expand, your knees feel light and spacious. The energy washes up your thighs, your hips and lower back, waves of soft light washing tension and worry from the muscles around your spine, your jaw, your face, your forehead, your eyes, your crown. A wave of relaxation cascading down your shoulders, your arms, flowing out your fingertips. Feel your body tingling, letting go, and taking on new dimensions.

A shimmering, diamond-bright pyramid rises around and above you. It glints with gold and tourmaline, moonstone, sapphire, ruby and amethyst. You are now held in a field of calm protection. You are safe and cared for, and all of your needs are met. Rest in this feeling for a moment, of being safe and cared for, of knowing that all of your needs are, and always will be, met.

A golden vortex opens before you, rotating slowly, rising through the top of the pyramid. It is a divine portal, ready to remove anything you no longer want to carry.

Purse your lips and breathe out slowly, but with some force, as if blowing out a row of candles. You will take five deep breaths this way.

With the first exhale, watch any remaining tension flowing out from all of your muscles. The tension leaves on the breath and is sent into the golden vortex, taken far, far away, never to return. Without thinking, without trying, simply notice what it looks like as it leaves you. Notice any sensations, memories, or thoughts that surface as you let it go.

With your second exhale, watch the excess fire and sparks of your nervous system flowing out on your stream of breath. Without thinking, without trying, notice what it looks like as it leaves you. This sparking energy streams directly into the vortex and is carried far, far away, never to return.

With your third exhale, watch as all density and stuckness lodged in all of your cells unsticks and flows out on the stream of your breath. Without thinking, without trying, notice what it looks like as it leaves you. This energy streams directly into the vortex and is carried far, far away, never to return.

With your fourth exhale, watch as all of the thoughts and stories of the outside world gather into one reservoir within you, and then flow out on the stream of your breath. Without thinking, without trying, notice what it looks like as it leaves you. This energy streams directly into the vortex and is carried far, far away, never to return.

With your final breath, let anything that is still left within you, anything you still want to let go of, come out on the stream of your breath. You do not have to know what it is; simply let it go. Without thinking, without trying, notice what it looks like as it leaves you. This energy streams directly into the vortex and is carried far, far away, never to return.

The vortex gently closes up, disappearing into a tiny pinprick of light. Then, all becomes dark and still.

Take a moment to rest in your body and notice the effect of this release.

(Pause and notice)

You are standing on a path in the crisp early morning, just before dawn. You can see only dimly the path winding in front of you. Your heart tells you this is the right path and that you are in the right place. Instinctively, you know that this path leads to the peak of a mountain. You know there is something waiting for you at the top, something more precious than you can understand. You do not know what the mountain, or its peak look like, but you know you must go there.

Every fiber in your being comes alive with longing for that which is at the top of this mountain, the end of this path. You want it so much that you stand on the edge of pain. You are plunged into the center of a raging confluence where pain, grief, desire, and ecstasy meet. Allow this feeling to course through your veins now. Allow it to open you with its magnitude.

(Pause and feel)

The feeling subsides, leaving behind a quiet determination, glowing calmly and resolutely in the center of your heart. You feel no fear as you step decisively onto the path in front of you.

The sun rises as you walk, bathing the landscape in new light, warming you delightfully after the chill of the dim predawn. You are grateful for this warmth and walk purposefully, without rushing, but without pausing either. You feel strong and capable, with the desire of the unknown mountaintop driving you forward. Look around. What do you see on this path? What does the landscape look like?

(Pause and notice)

You walk a long way. The path becomes very rocky and very steep. You scramble up rocks that are cold and slippery under your hands. You come to a sheer rockface and without hesitating, you begin to climb.

You are now high above the stones below, but you remember the bridge you had created before out of thin air. You know there is nothing to fear. Calmly you find handholds and footholds that seem to appear whenever you need them. You become tired, but you breathe loving, golden light into your arms, your legs. Your muscles ache with strain, but you push onwards. Again and again you find strength that you didn't know you possessed. You find this strength to be surprisingly effortless, even as your muscles quake. You move upwards without doubt or fear.

You know you cannot go back down. You cannot turn back. You can only continue onwards and upwards. You bring your focus into the present moment, breathing an aureole of light around your body. Your entire life becomes concentrated into a single point- one handhold, one foothold, then the next. In this way, you climb up the cliff and soon are grasping the top of the rock face. You haul yourself up and over the edge, and lay for a moment on the ground, breathing and resting. When you have rested, you continue on.

Presently you come to a vast, raging river. The water is running high and fast. You know it could close over your head instantly if you stepped in. You feel the heaviness of fear descend on you, and you stand at the bank for a moment, considering.

You do not for a moment consider turning back. You think instead about how to get across this river. You feel urgency and drive to ford it, but there is no bridge. Your heart soothes you, and you listen. Your heart says, "wait."

You make camp by the side of the river and wait. Days go by, and you become impatient. Still your heart says, "wait." You devise many schemes, you throw stones into the river to see if you can make a bridge. You try making a rope out of toughened grasses; you walk up and down and up and down the bank and find no place where it narrows, you find no bridge. Always you come back to the place of the crossing and voice of your heart. "Wait," it says.

So you wait.

You find the waiting more difficult than climbing the rockface, when all of life was action and focus. In the stillness of this waiting, when nothing seems to be happening, voices rise up within you. These are jeering voices, judgmental voices. They say all of the things that you fear. By the banks of this river, you feel as though you are nowhere, you are no one. You are in between. Not moving and yet, not giving up. In these long, listless days you question everything. You question every choice you have ever made. You wonder if the cruel, jeering voices are telling the truth. You wonder if this is the right path. You wonder what you were ever thinking to start out on something so unknown. You think about all of the things you could have had, the lives you could have lived had you chosen differently. You wonder if you will be stuck here forever. In the safety of this moment, let those voices rise up so you can recognize them in the future. What do they say? What do they sound like? As you listen, know that they are not the truth.

(Pause and listen)

One day you retrace your steps back down the path that you had walked so long ago. You find it overgrown and inhospitable, no longer accommodating your steps. You know now that turning back is impossible. The way has closed behind you.

Some days, by the implacable river, you cry out in desperate anger and frustration. Some days you lie lifeless and discouraged, unable even to stand. Some days you make games out of stones and talk to the birds that land nearby. In the safety of this moment, let all of these feelings rise up so you can recognize them in the future and know they have no power over you. Let these feelings sweep through you and release.

(Pause and feel)

One day, after many days of waiting, you notice that the river is lower, and slower than it was. Hope flares in you, but you suppress it quickly, not daring to believe that, after so much time, you may be able to continue forward. You have almost forgotten why you are here. There is something tempting about staying here, by the riverbank, forever.

Over the course of the next long, sunny days the river loses its force and turbulence. Then one day your heart says, "now."

The image of the mountaintop kindles back in your heart. You remember, and longing sears you once more. You have to know what is at the top. You gather your things and walk easily across, splashing as you go.

After some time, you come to a place where the path splits. You must choose, right or left. You do not know where these paths lead. You turn into your heart. It tells you all paths lead to the top of the mountain, and that you cannot make a wrong choice. You choose. Which direction do you choose?

Sometimes as you walk, you come across other travelers, their paths crossing with your own. Some question you, asking if you have ever been to the top of the mountain, trying to understand why you must go there if you have never seen it. You cannot explain, and the explanations take too much of your time. These travelers throw you into doubt. You learn to avoid these travelers. You remain pleasant but quiet, sharing nothing of your plans. You continue moving.

Some travelers are helpful. Sometimes their paths align with yours for a time, and you walk together. You are sometimes tempted to join these travelers on *their* paths. Their paths seem more exciting than yours, and you yearn for company, as your path can feel very lonely at times. Each time you try to cross over to a path that is not yours, however, you become lost and dissatisfied. Sometimes, when you step back onto your path and leave the other travelers, they react poorly, calling you names. You learn to let go and forgive yourself for straying. You learn not to listen to any voice that does not harmonize with the voice of your heart.

You learn to stay to your path, to let the other travelers come and go as they need to and as their paths allow. Your path is your very own. It is the constant thread that leads you onwards.

You walk and walk. For years you walk. Sometimes you reach a summit, or a nice place to rest, and you think "this must be it," and you stop. You try to make a home here. Deep down, though, you know it is not the place, it is not the summit, it is not your home. Eventually, and sometimes with much heartbreak, you leave that place behind, that place that was not home. You do not know what is at the top of the mountain, but you know you will *know* it when you arrive.

Over time you notice that you are changing. Your body changes and, with trepidation and some grief, you allow it to change. You become like an animal walking through its natural habitat. As this happens, the path becomes smoother, the clamoring voices become quieter, the way becomes easier, the obstacles less difficult to surmount. You become more and more certain of yourself and your steps. You know, when this happens, that you are nearing your destination. You look down at your body now, so different from the form that set out on this path. You do not recognize that person any longer as you. What do you look like now? What does it feel like to be you, in your natural habitat, treading the clear and narrow path to your apex?

Take time now to continue walking along the path. Notice what arrives, what, or whom, emerges in front of you. Possibly you receive messages, wisdom, downloads as you walk.

(Pause, listen, and notice)

At last, you behold the peak of your mountain, the peak you have been seeking for so long. You have spent so many hours imagining it, but it looks different than you imagined. What does it look like?

(Pause to notice)

You know now you are close, but you have learned patience. There is still ground to cover. Here, towards the top, the path dissolves and you see there are hundreds and hundreds of ways you can reach the summit. Your heart guides you, step by step. Somehow you know that the obstacles have all been removed, and that the way in front of you is clear and easy. You do not celebrate yet, however. After all this time, you can hardly dare to hope that the final few steps will be easy.

Finally, you take the final step and behold the summit. Someone, or something, is waiting for you there. It is that which has driven you forward, day after day, year after year. It is the thing you have dreamed of, hoped for, imagined, longed for. It is the deepest, unspoken yearning of your tender heart. What is it? Run to it now. Bring it into your heart. Take time to be with it. Let it speak to you.

(Long pause to listen)

It is now time to bring this feeling of completion and rest, into your waking life. Breathing deeply, you bring the light of deep contentment into your lungs, into your belly, and into your heart. Contentment flows from your heart into every cell of your body.

Keeping your eyes closed, become aware of your physical body. Bring movement into your fingers, your toes, your ankles, your shoulders. With eyes still closed, raise your right hand, and gently but firmly tap your sternum, and anywhere else that feels good, to imprint these feelings, these messages, into your body.

Still resting in this feeling of deep and abiding contentment, open your eyes. Remain this way for a few moments as you take in your surroundings.

And gradually, when you're ready, move back into your waking life.

Before you engage in any practical tasks, take time to journal, write, or create a voice recording to reflect on what you experienced. Note how you feel, and what has changed for you. This act of reflection will even more firmly imprint the experience into your body.

Conclusion

You have been seeking, I know. It has been a long, hard road of seeking. It has been a time of blind stumbling, of weariness, of dead-end paths and fitful restlessness. You have suffered and touched the depth of your suffering, not once, but again and again. You have plumbed your own darkness with courage and resilience and devotion, diving into the deeps once more, and once more again, just to make sure there was nothing left to bring to the surface.

I know the number of times you have stared at the jagged peak of yet another mountain, your enthusiasm flagging at the thought of another climb. I know the weariness that has seeped into your bones. Another peak. Another climb. Another false summit. Another dogged journey.

You have felt the wind on your face and the Earth under your feet. Sometimes, you have felt her under your knees. You have sunk your hands into her damp body and wept until there was nothing left. Your muscles have grown hard and strong with climbing, your face marked with the character and strength that comes with stumbling and moving forward. You have learned the lessons that come with loss and grief. You have shouldered the mantle of your choices. You have let your heart break and open, and open and break again until it has become one continuous stream, the breaking and the opening merging into one, the natural heartbeat of love and loss.

In this courageous and determined seeking, in your relentless plumbing of depths, in the resolute taking on of shadow after shadow, fear after fear, you may have forgotten why you began it all in the first place. You may have forgotten the point of your seeking, your climbing, your suffering, your growth.

You did not come here to fight eternal shadows. You did not come here to climb endless mountains. You came here to shine your bright and exuberant light into the world. You came here to rest, at last, in joy.

It is time now to claim that joy.

You have not known a life without battle, without something to conquer, to confront, to prove. To *do*. But I tell you, that life you have known is over. You have found what you are seeking. You have been lifted into the place beyond proving, beyond seeking, beyond knowing.

And so, your final act of courage, your final sovereign choice will be to accept that the life you have known is over, and to open to the dawn that is even now upon you. The fighting, the seeking, the striving, the climbing and endless, wearying journey is at an end.

It is time to trust that you are complete. You are whole. You have found all you need to find; you have fulfilled all you need to fulfill; you have suffered all you needed to suffer.

It is time now to harvest the fruits of your suffering, your searching, your courageous growth. It is time to rest in the soft and welcoming dawn of a new life, one of abundance and wellbeing, one of generosity and peace and celebration and endless empowerment. It is time to dance in the light of your breaking dawn. It is time to trust that all you have ever wanted is coming to pass. You do not need to earn it. You do not need to prove yourself worthy. You do not need to strive or change or grow or fight. You do not need to seek anymore. You need only to open and receive. You need only to rest, at last, in the gentle embrace of your eternal garden: the unchanging, indwelling Eden of your perfect heart.

Be still now, and know that you are God.

References

Aboulker-Muscat, C. (1997). *Mea culpa: Tales of resurrection.* ACMI Press.

Gibran, K. (1923/2017). *The prophet.* Prakash Books.

Melchizedek, D. (2011). *Earth/Sky/Heart Workshop* [video]. Gaia. Retrieved from: https://www.gaia.com/series/earthskyheart-workshop

Milton, J. (1667/2000). *Paradise lost.* Penguin Books.

Székely, Edmond B. (1977). *The Essene gospel of peace. Book one: the Aramaic and old Slavonic texts.* Academy Books.

Yeats, W.B. (1956). *The collected poems of W.B. Yeats.* "Sailing to Byzantium" (1926); "The Second Coming" (1919); "Song of Wandering Aengus" (1897). Macmillan Press.

About the Author
Dr. Katherine Hall Newburgh, Ph.D. (Kate)
Author of *The New Eden: Paradise Retold* and her memoir, *Finding Home*
Founder of Books of Eden Publishing.

Kate at the summit of Mount Schiehallion,
Fairy Mountain of the Caledonians.

Dr. Katherine Hall Newburgh, Ph. D (Kate) is the author of several books, including *The New Eden: Paradise Retold* and her award-winning memoir, *Finding Home*. She is also the author of Annea'rah Speaks: A Tale of Creation as Told by the Fae, published under Katherine Hall. She is the founder of Books of Eden Publishing, LLC, which offers to the world a new genre: Pedagogy of the Divine. Kate believes that this world we live in is magical beyond understanding, and her greatest joy (apart from playing with horses, being in nature, traveling, singing songs, and making up ad-hoc ceremonies) is sharing this belief with everyone she meets. Learn more about Kate, her books, and her work at www.booksofeden.com.

www.ingramcontent.com/pod-product-compliance
Lightning Source LLC
Chambersburg PA
CBHW032224080426
42735CB00008B/697